Outline *for a* Comparative Grammar *of some* Algonquian Languages*

*Ojibway, Cree, Micmac, Natick [Massachusett], and Blackfoot

C.C. Uhlenbeck

Translated from the original Dutch by Joshua Jacob Snider

OUTLINE FOR A COMPARATIVE GRAMMAR OF SOME
ALGONQUIAN LANGUAGES: OJIBWAY, CREE, MICMAC, NATICK
[MASSACHUSETT] AND BLACKFOOT
   C.C. UHLENBECK

Translated from the original Dutch
"Ontwerp van eene vergelijkende vormleer van eenige
Algonkin-talen"

Verhandelingen der Koninklijke Akademie van Wetenschappen te
Amsterdam.

Afdeeling Letterkunde. Deel 11 No. 3 Amsterdam, Johannes
Müller.1910

by Joshua Jacob Snider

With permission from **The Royal Academy of Arts and Sciences in Amsterdam.**
With additional notes.

OUTLINE FOR A COMPARATIVE GRAMMAR OF SOME
ALGONQUIAN LANGUAGES: OJIBWAY, CREE, MICMAC, NATICK
[MASSACHUSETT] AND BLACKFOOT
  by C.C. UHLENBECK
  translated by JOSHUA JACOB SNIDER

Copyright © 2013 by Joshua Jacob Snider
Mundart Press, Petoskey MI.
ISBN: Soft Cover 978-0-615-38402-3

All rights reserved. No part of this book may be reproduced or transmitted in any form or by any means, electronic or mechanical, including photocopying, recording or by any information storage and retrieval system, without permission in writing from the publisher.

Library of Congress Control Number: 2010941794
1. Algonquian languages-Bibliography. 2. Algonquian languages-Etymology. 3. Algonquian languages-Grammar, Comparative. 4. Algonkian. 5. Algic languages.

Translation in loving memory of
Elliott Joseph 'E.J.' Hughes
4/21/1979 - 4/22/2006

Also by
Joshua Jacob Snider

A Bear Took Flight. From the original Yiddish *"A ber iz gefloygn"* by Itzik Kipnis, Cooperative Publishing House Culture League Kiev 1924 State Trust "Kiev Press".

Months and Days. By Itzik Kipnis 1926. Forthcoming translation.

Translator's preface

I would first like to thank my wife Sarah for her patience and support in my time consuming endeavors. I also wish to thank the following people. For encouraging me to undertake this project, Manna McGrew, who also helped me a great deal in the earliest stages of the translation. Mary Eggermont-Molenaar, for the many hours she spent going through and correcting my work, her importance in this project could not be overstated. Inge Genee, for help with translation. Ives Goddard, for encouragement, pointing out errors, answering questions on all of the languages, and for pointing me in the right direction for most of my additional resources. Roger (F.R.) Higgins, for additional help with Massachusett and for bringing Audrey Dawe's work on Micmac to my attention. Joe Wilmot, for help with Mi'gmaw. My sister, Deborah (Nolan) Rogoschensky of the First Nation Missinabie Cree Band, for typing the original rough draft of my handwritten translation. Drew Cherven and the Petoskey Public Library, for diligently seeking all of the resources I requested. Kenny Pheasant and his dedication to Ojibwe's sister language, Odawa ((A)-Nishnabemowin) (See Valentine 2001, Cappel 2006 and Kiogima 2010). Alice (Gasko) Hughes of the Little Traverse Bay Bands of Odawa Indians, for making sure her son Elliot had interaction with her ancestral language and Elliot and her in turn for sharing that with me.

I have added much supplemental material to the translation of Uhlenbeck's text in the hopes that it will create a somewhat more fleshed out view of the grammars being treated here. These additions are indicated with swords in the text.

I have not used s/he where Uhlenbeck used only hij 'he' etc., but it should be known that in these cases the third person does not distinguish between male and female.

Concerning orthography I have reproduced all symbols according to the original Dutch version. For orthography of the supplemental material I have reproduced the orthography of my source except in the rare cases where I have not been able to reproduce the symbols employed by the source. In one case I have normalized one Natick (Massachusett) letter to agree with Uhlenbeck's transcription.

These cases are that for the Massachusett from G&B 1988 I have used the Greek symbol ω (î represents this same sound) regularly after

Uhlenbeck where G&B 1988 gives the symbol 8 for this letter. I have used an ᵉ and ₑ after Goddard. According to Goddard the ₑ could be written as plain old *y*, but tᵉ, written as *ch* by some writers, is as in British "tune", i.e. "tyune".

For Mi'gmaw î has been used to indicate a barred ɨ.

A disclaimer should be made on the forms presented here. The forms that I have added are from many different sources and dialects. Even Uhlenbeck's 1938 Blackfoot grammar is a different dialect than the one treated here in this earlier work. In this work Uhlenbeck has also used such forms for Ojibway as nin-wābama 'I see him' etc. although before a w- the prefix would only be ni-. This may be due to Baraga writing (nin-) by itself after words in his notation, but let it serve as a caution to the reader that at least some of the forms in this work are abstractions.

At this point I would like to include a short list of suggested reading. This list includes some short descriptions of contents as well (for full citations see *bibliography for further reading*).

- Bloomfield's Algonquian (comparative grammar of five Central Algonquian dialects) and his paper On the Sound System of Central Algonquian (phonetic shifts in five central dialects).
- Michelson's Phonetic Shifts in Algonquian Languages (phonetic shifts for Plains Algonquian languages including Blackfoot and dialects more characteristic of that branch such as Arapaho and Cheyenne, as well as phonetic shifts for the Central and Eastern Branches of the Algonquain family.
- Forbes' Wapanakamikok Language Relationships (this work is of a different character than the others. It is of a type where things such as folk etymologies are more acceptable than they are in more traditional scientific linguistic materials. The work is more cultural and slightly mnemonic in nature and attempts to approach Pan-Algonquian language issues from a Native perspective).
- Swan's Algonquian Spirit (translations from all three branches of the language family [around eighteen or so dialects]).
- Goddard's The Historical Origins of Cheyenne Inflections.
- Waldman and Braun's Word Dance (this work gives etymologies for many words concerning the Algonquiian languages).
- Uhlenbeck's Some word-comparisons between Blackfoot and other Algonquian languages and Additional Blackfoot-Arapaho comparisons. For an exhaustive bibliography and account of Uhlenbeck's works and

efforts see Genee, Inge and Hinrichs' C.C. Uhlenbeck (1866-1951): A linguist revisited.

Further reading on Blackfoot Grammar:

- Frantz' *Blackfoot Grammar*.
- Holterman's *A Blackfoot Language Study*.
- Taylor's *A Grammar of Blackfoot*.

It is still my hope that one day a comparative Algonquian grammar will be bound together with a reader like those texts that are currently available for many other language families, but for now I hope that this piece will be of some help and perhaps fill a gap.

Any and all remaining errors in this text are my own.

Petoskey (Pet-o-se-ga), MI, May 2010
Joshua Jacob Snider

Translator's bibliography

Baraga, Frederic. 1878-80. *A Dictionary of the Ojibway Language.* Minnesota Historical Society. 1992 reprint. Originaly published as A Dictionary of the Otchipwe Language 1878-80 Beauchemin & Valois, Montreal.

Bloomfield, Leonard. 1946. *Algonquian* pp 85-129 in Linguistic Structures of Native America, Cornelius Osgood, ed., Viking Fund Publications in Anthropology No. 6, New York.

Cappel, Constance. ed. 2006. *Odawa Language and Legends: Andrew J. Blackbird and Raymond Kiogima.* Xlibris.

Dawe, Audrey. 1986. *The Fundamentals of Micmac Historical Morphology.* M.A. Thesis, Department of Linguistics, Memorial University of Newfoundland. St. John's, Newfoundland.

Delisle, Gilles L. and Emanuel L. Metalic. 1976. *Micmac Teaching Grammar (Preliminary Version)*, Thunderbird Press, Quebec.

Eggermont-Molenaar, Mary. ed. 2005. *Montana 1911; A Professor and His Wife Among the Blackfeet.* Calgary/Lincoln: University of Calgary Press/ University of Nebraska Press.

Goddard, Ives. 1983. *The Eastern Algonquian Subordinative Mode and the Importance of Morphology.* International Journal of American Linguistics 49.4: 351-387.

Goddard, Ives and Kathleen J. Bragdon. 1988. *Native Writings in Massachusett Vol 2* (grammar), Memoirs of the American Philosophical Society; 185, The American Philosophical Society, Philidelphia. (G&B 1988)

Goddard, Ives. 2007. *Reconstruction of the Independent Indicative.* pp. 207-271 In "Papers of the 38th Algonquian Conference, ed. H.C. Wolfart (University of Manitoba, Winipeg).

Hewson, John and Bernard Francis. 1990. *The Micmac Grammar of Father Pacifique.* In Algonquian and Iriquoian Linguistics, Memoir; 7, Manitoba, Winipeg. (H&F 1990)

Inglis, Stephanie and Eleanor Johnson. 2001. *The Mi'kmaq Future: An Analysis by Stephanie Inglis and Eleanor Johnson* pp. 249-257, Mi'kmaq Studies, University College of Cape Breton. In "Papers of the 32nd Algonquian Conference. Vol. 32.

Kiogima, Raymond. 2010. *The Complete Odawa Language.* Raymond Kiogima, Harbor Springs, Michigan.

Proulx, Paul Martin. 1978. *Micmac Inflection.* Ph.D. disertation. Cornell University.

Uhlenbeck, C. C. 1938. *A Concise Blackfoot Grammar Based on Material from the Southern Peigans.* N.V. Noord-Hollandsche Uitgevers-Maatschappij, 240 p. (Verhandelingen der Koninklijke Akademie van Wetenschappen, Afdeeling Letterkunde, N. R. 41). Reprinted Ca. 1978-1984 = no. 486.

———. 1910. *Ontwerp van een vergelijkende vormleer van eenige Algonkin-talen.* Johannes Müller (Verhandelingen der Koninklijke Akademie van Wetenschappen, Afdeeling Letterkunde, N.R., 11/3).

Vallentine, J. R. 2001. *Nishnaabemwin Reference Grammar.* University of Toronto Press, Toronto.

Bibliography for further reading.

Bloomfield, Leonard. 1946. *Algonquian* (see translator's bibliography).

Bloomfield, Leonard. 1925 (Dec.). *On the Sound System of Central Algonquian.* Language vol.I number 4, pp 130-156.

Forbes, Jack D. 1972. *Wapanakamikok Language Relationships: An Introductory Study of the Mutual Intelligibility Among the Powhatan, Lenape, Natick, Nanticoke and Otchipwe Languages.* Native American Studies, Tecumseh Center, University of California, Davis, California.

Frantz, Donald G. 1991. *Blackfoot Grammar.* University of Toronto Press.

Genee, Inge and Jan Paul Hinrichs. ed. 2008/2009. *C.C. Uhlenbeck (1866-1951): A linguist revisited.* Canadian Journal of Netherlandic Studies, XXIX, ii / XXX, i (Fall 2008 / Spring 2009).

Goddard, Ives. 2000. *The Historical Origins of Cheyenne Inflections.* pp. 77-129. "Papers of the 31st Algonquian Conference" Vol 31 Vol 31 31:77-129.

Holterman, Jack. 1996. *A Blackfoot Language Study; A Special Study of the Blackfoot Language on the Blackfeet Indian Reservation, 1932-1996*. Piegan Institute, Browning, Montana.

Michelson, Truman. 1935 (August). *Phonetic Shifts in Algonquian Languages.* pp131-171 in the "International Journal of American Linguistics" volume VIII Numbers 3-4.

Swan, Brian. ed. 2005. *Algonquian Spirit: Contemporary Translations of the Algonquian Literatures of North America*, University of Nebraska Press.

Taylor, Alan Ross. 1953. *A Grammar of Blackfoot*. Ph.D Dissertation University of California, Berkley.

Uhlenbeck, C. C. 1925. *Some word-comparisons between Blackfoot and other Algonquian languages.* International Journal of American Linguistics 3:103-108.

——. 1927. *Additional Blackfoot-Arapaho comparisons.* International Journal for American Linguistics 4:227-228

Waldman, Carl and Moly Braun. 1994. *Word Dance: The Language of Native American Culture.* Facts on File, Inc. an Infobase Holdings Company.

Outline *for a* Comparative Grammar *of some* Algonquian Languages*

*Ojibway, Cree, Micmac, Natick [Massachusett], and Blackfoot

C.C. Uhlenbeck

Translated from the original Dutch by Joshua Jacob Snider

Preface

It would seem that circumstances shall, with the passage of time, permit me to delve deeper into the study of the Algonquian languages than that which is possible from my office. Still I think that for the moment this sketch, though quite imperfect and incomplete, may be of some use to students of the North American languages. Nowhere can one find a comparative description of this language group that contains anything more than the most elementary, or that presents anything more than juxtaposition without an historical perspective. I do not imagine that I have accomplished a great deal in this direction, but I am quite confident of the scarce results that I have obtained. In general, my outline bears a more descriptive than historical character, although I can see well that the reconstruction of history is the goal that we must strive towards. Only if we can form an idea of the Algonquian language family for ourselves first, will it then become possible to embark on an investigation into the potential relationship with other language families.

The languages that I have compared in this outline are Ojibway, Cree, Micmac, Natick and Blackfoot. (I have employed the initial letters of these language names as abbreviations). Only occasionally have I consulted other dialects. I am well aware that the choice of five out of perhaps fifty dialects is not defensible in all respects, but I had to make a choice: whether to limit myself to a few languages and deliver something workable or to completely abandon devising a comparative grammar.

I have taken my material from the following works:

Bishop Baraga. *A theoretical and practical grammar of the Otchipwe language* (2), Montreal 1878.

E. F. Wilson. *The Ojebway language*, Toronto 1874.

A. Lacombe. *Dictionnaire de la langue des Cris*, Montréal 1874.

J. Horden. *A grammar of the Cree language*, London 1881.

Abbé Maillard. *Grammaire de la langue Mikmaque, redigée et mise en ordre par J. M. Bellenger Ptre*, New-York 1864.

S. T. Rand. *Dictionary of the language of the Micmac Indians*, Halifax N.S. 1888.

J. Eliot. *A grammar of the Massachusetts Indian language. A new edition by P. S. du Ponceau and an introduction and supplementary observations by J. Pickering, Boston 1822.*

J. H. Trumbull. *Natick dictionary*, Washington 1903.

J. W. Tims. *Grammar and dictionary of the Blackfoot language in the dominion of Canada*, London 1889.

I have also made some additional use of:

F. Müller. *Der grammatische bau der Algonkin-sprachen*, Wien 1867.

R. Sowa. *Die Nominalbildung in den Algonkin-sprachen*, Brünn 1891.

H. R. Schoolcraft. *An essay on the grammatical structure of the Algonquin language (Information respecting the history... of the Indian tribes II, 351 sqq.).*

Th. Hurburt. *A memoir on the inflections of the Chippewa tongue (Information respecting the history... of the Indian tribes IV, 385 sqq.).*

N. O. (J. A. Cuoq). *Etudes philologiques sur quelques langues sauvages de l'Amérique*, Montréal 1866.

L. Adam. *Esquisse d'une grammaire camparée des dialectes Cree et Chippeway*, Paris 1876.

——. *Examen grammatical comparée de seize langues américaines*, **Paris 1878.**

Unfortunately I have been unable to get my hands on J. Howse's, *Grammar of the Cree language, with analysis of the Chippeway dialect*, London 1865.

I do not have many remarks concerning spelling. I have attempted to give consistent representation to the transcription of sounds. Therefore, I have also used the symbols *š, ž, tš* and *dž* which should not cause any misunderstanding, and in Blackfoot I write *ks* where Tims employs both *x* as well as *ks*. After all, according to his own words it is not to be doubted that by *x* he means the combination of *k* and *s*. In my writing, there is decidedly much inconsistency in vowel quantity, but this could not be avoided because of the inadequacy of my sources. I point out in particular that I never provide a length sign for the *e* of Cree, although for the most part it does not appear to differ from the *ē* of Ojibway. Naturally, I have not altered the spelling of Natick. After all, it would be irresponsible to tamper with material that has been handed down from the seventeenth century. In cases of doubt, I have not dared to alter the spelling in the remaining dialects.

Leiden, May 1909
C. C. Uhlenbeck

Table Of Contents†

	Pg.
Preface	[iii]

I. Nouns

General remarks (§1)	[1]
Stem classes (§2)	[1]
Gender (§3-§4)	[3]
Number (§5-§6)	[4]
Case (§7-§9)	[6]
Subordinate forms (§10-§11)	[9]
Possessive inflections (§12-§16)	[11]
Temporal inflection (§17)	[19]
Noun forming suffixes (§18-§19)	[20]
Adjectives (§20)	[24]
Numerals (§21-§22)	[26]

II. Pronouns

General remarks (§23)	[29]
Personal possessive pronouns (§24)	[30]
Other pronouns (§25-§28)	[31]

III. Verbs

General remarks (§29)	[35]
Mutation (§30-§32)	[36]
Distribution of verbs (§36-§45)	[38]
Verbal types (§34-§35)	[41]
Mood representation (§36-§45)	[42]
Tenses (§46-§48)	[59]
Incorporation (§49)	[62]
Secondary verbs (§50)	[65]

---

† The *Table of Contents* is a translation of the Dutch original and corresponds to the original Dutch. The pagination of the original Dutch is indicated in the body of this text.

[1] 1. Nouns

General remarks

§ 1. Algonquian, which lacks the distinction between masculine and feminine genders, has two genders[a] that are commonly indicated by the names **living** and **lifeless**, but that I will rather call **animate** and **inanimate**, because these terms are easily abbreviated as **a.** and **i.**.

There are no duals present in the noun, but as a rule the singular and plural are clearly distinguished from each other. The grammatical cases are shown by syntactic means, but in some Algonquian languages there is a locative characterized by a suffix. Noteworthy is the presence of the subordinative forms (obviative and subobviative)[b] in Ojibway, Cree and other dialects. We must assume that where we do not find such forms, they have been lost.

The substantives also have a possessive, and to a certain degree also a temporal inflection.

A peculiarity of Blackfoot is the presence of relative nominal forms characterized by a -*k* suffix, which are used in conjunction with the relative pronouns.

The remarks above only apply to nouns. The special rules, which apply to the adjectives and numerals, shall be discussed in the last three paragraphs of this chapter.

Stem classes

§ 2. In Ojibway, the nominal stems can be divided into two main groups:
(A) Stems ending in a vowel, which is retained in all forms.
(B) Stems ending in a vowel or sound group, which is lost in the common singular, but preserved before a suffix and in compounds. This class can be divided again into the following subdivisions: α) stems in -*a*-, β) stems in -*ia*-, γ) stems in -*wa*-, δ) stems in -*i*- and ε) stems in -*o*-.

Examples of class (A):
- *ogimā* 'chief', pl. *ogimāg*.
- *anišinābe* 'native', pl. *anišinābeg*.

- *animikī* 'thunder', pl. *animikīg*.
- *abwi* 'paddle', pl. *abwīn*.
- *windigo* 'giant', pl. *windigog*.

  Examples of class (B):
- α) stems in *-a-*:
  kokōš 'pig', obv. *kokōšan*, pl. *kokōšag*.
  kitigān 'field', pl. *kitigānan*.
- β) stems in *-ia-*:
  mišikē 'turtle', obv. *mišikēian*, pl. *mišikēiag*.
- γ) stems in *-wa-*:
  inini 'man' obv. *ininiwan*, pl. *ininiwag*.
  odēna 'village' pl.*odēnawan*.
- δ) stems in *-i-*:
  asīn 'stone', obv. *asīnin*, pl. *asīnig*, cf. *asini-wakaigan* 'stone house'.
  mitigwāb 'bow (and arrow)', pl. *mitigwābin*.
- ε) stems in *-o-*:
  mitig 'tree', obv. *mitigon*., pl. *mitigog* cf. *mitigo-wakaigan* 'log (wood) house'.
  wāwan 'egg' pl. *wāwanon*.

The participles (personal gerunds) in *-d* also belong to subdivision δ) of class (B), but the *-d* changes to a *-dž-* before an *-i-* e.g., *enamiād* 'he (she) who prays'{c} pl. *enamiādžig*. In some dialects, the older form in *-dig* has been preserved.

In the locative, we do not always find the vocalism that we would expect based on the plural form. (e.g.) *kitigān* 'field' has the locative *kitigāning* although the plural is *kitigānan*. Another example is *odēna* 'village', loc. *odēnang*, pl. *odēnawan*. Forms such as *kitigāning* and *odēnang* can probably be explained by influence from the other stems. Also, in certain cases where the stem vowels turn up in the diminutive and the pejorative, the original situation has by no means always been preserved.

That the final vowel is lost here and preserved there is surely on account of the old accent conditions. The same phenomenon can be observed in the conjugation: after all *ikkito* 'he (she) says' stands in contrast to *nind-ikkit* 'I say' and *kid-ikkit* 'you say', and it can be seen from the negative forms *nind-ikkito-si* and *kid-ikkito-si* that these forms were once *nind-ikkito* and *kid-ikkito*. This is also the case for *bōsi* 'he (she) embarks': *nin-bōs* 'I embark', *ki-bōs*' you embark' (negatives *nin-bōsi-si, ki-bōsi-si*).

[3]

In Cree, we also find the classes *A.* and *B.*, but the subdivisions of class *B.* have been reduced to two, because -*a*- and -*wa*- (-*wo*) have replaced the other stem-vowels, except for certain stem-vowels in the locative and possessive inflections. Sometimes, however, a word belongs to class *A.* in Cree while the stem-vowel has been lost in Ojibway e.g., C. *asini*, O. *asīn* 'stone'; C. *kona*, O.*gōn* 'snow'. Cree is more archaic than Ojibway in yet another respect, namely in the singular form of words that exhibit a -*wa*- stem in Ojibway, like O. *migizi* 'eagle', pl.*migiziwag*, C. *mikisiw*, pl. *mikisiwok* and O. *ikwē* 'woman', pl. *ikwēwag*, C. *iskwew*, pl. *iskwewok*. We see that the final *w* of the Cree words is a remnant of the soundgroup -*wa*- (-*wo*-) which is completely preserved in the plural. However, we also find this *w* in Cree where Ojibway has an -*ia*- stem e.g., O. *nižodē* 'twin', pl. *nižodēiag*, C.*nižotew, nižotewok,* in which case the presence of this consonant can not be so easily judged. That this *w* appears in such words probably has its explanation in the -*wa*- stems spreading outside of their original domain. Cree still has traces of the old stem-vowel in the locative e.g., *askikok* 'in the kettle' (O. *akikong*). It is noteworthy that the locatives of Cree and Ojibway are sometimes vocalized in the same manner while the plural of Ojibway exhibits another vowel e.g., C. *mikiwamik*, O. *wigawāming* 'in the house (wigwam)': O. *wigiwāman* 'wigwams'.

The original stem-vowels of class *B.* are better preserved in Micmac and Natick, but in Blackfoot the old conditions are no longer recognizable.

Gender

§ 3. As I have already said, the substantives of Algonquian fall into two genders: **animate** or **living** and **inanimate** or **lifeless**. To the animate gender belong not only living creatures but also numerous words that are only animate in the animistic imagination of the Indian. {d} In Ojibway just as in Cree for example: sun, moon, star, thunder, snow, ice, stone, silver, kettle, pipe, tobacco, bread, sled, clock and ribbon are considered living (animate). The names of trees and plants are usually considered to belong to the animate gender, but strangely enough they are considered to belong to the lifeless (inanimate) gender in Natick. As a rule, the names of body parts are inanimate in Algonquian and the same applies to many words that indicate parts of trees and plants, but in Ojibway for instance, thorn, [4] raspberry, apple, and potato as well as corn-ear and corn-stalk - like corn itself - are animate. A close inquiry into the distribution of the words in both of the genders for the various Algonquian languages would undoubtedly provide surprising results. Especially interesting are such cases where one language differs from another, such as paddle and spoon, which are animate in Cree and inanimate in Ojibway.

§ 4. Outside of the syntactic context, the gender to which a substantive belongs appears clearly in the common, as well as in the possessive inflection of the plural formation. Furthermore, the use of the subordinate forms is also chiefly, though not completely, limited to the animate gender, by which means we also have found a criterion in certain cases. In the sentence, the gender can be recognized by agreement, although this is not applied to the same extent in all of the various languages. In Natick and also to a certain extent in Micmac, the attributive adjective agrees with the gender of the substantive to which it belongs, while this is not the case in the other languages we are treating here. In Algonquian, one uses verb forms in place of predicative adjectives, which agree with the subject in gender just as the other intransitive verbs do. In contrast, the transitive verbs agree in gender with their direct object. There are still other cases of agreement, but that which I have already said is sufficient to give an idea of the significant role that the distinction of the two genders fulfills in the Algonquian languages. I only mention here that the distinction between animate and inanimate is also present in the pronouns.

Number

§ 5. The singular does not have a special inflection and the dual is lacking not only for the noun but also - apart from Micmac, which possesses dual verbal forms - in the remaining parts of speech for the languages treated here. The **plural** varies according to the gender. The plural inflections for the animate words are O. *-g*, C. *-k*, M. *-k*, N. *-g* and B. *-ks*.[1] With regard to the inanimate gender, Ojibway forms

---

1. Nasalization does occur in Natick from the contraction of word final |-ī| + |-ak| giving |-onk| Goddard &Bragdon 1988. This process is again treated under §13 third person plural (plural noun).

the plural with an *-n* suffix to which an *-l* corresponds in Micmac.[2] Cree has actually lost the *-n* plural inflection. In Natick the plural of the inanimate gender ends in *-sh* and in Blackfoot it ends in *-sts*.

For the animate words of class *A.* in Ojibway and Cree, and as well as for the inanimate words of this class in Ojibway, we find the plural inflection immediately following the preserved vowel everywhere. This is also the case for class *B* in Ojibway where the subdivisions of this group stand out sharply from each other through quite differing vocalizations (*-a-*, *-ia-*, *-wa-*, *-i-* and *-o-*), while in Cree *-a-* and *-wa-* (*-wo*) have spread at the expense of other vowels. Since the plural inflection *-n* has been lost in Cree it appears that the plural of inanimate words is formed by the means of the actually thematic *-a* and *-wa*. In Micmac we sometimes find the stem vowels *-a-*, *-e-*, *-i-* and *-u-* before the plural suffix and words in *-t* have a pl. in *-gi-k*. In Natick, the *-g* of the animate gender is always preceded with an *-o-* (although, sometimes after a remaining preserved original vowel) or *-wo* and the *sh* of the inanimate gender is always preceded by an *-a-* or *-wa-* (*-ana-* or *-wana*). In Blackfoot an *ĕ* or an *ĭ* often precedes the plural suffixes.

Examples of the animate gender:

- O. *mēme* 'woodpecker', pl. *mēmeg*.
- O. *wagoš* 'fox', pl. *wagošag*.
- O. *opīn* 'potato', pl. *opīnig*.
- O. *anāng* 'star' pl. *anāngog*.
- C. *niska* 'bustard',{e}[3] pl. *niskak*.
- C. *pakkwežigan* 'bread', pl. *pakkwežiganak*. (O. *pakwēžigan*, pl. *pakwēžiganak*).
- C. *mistik* 'tree', pl. *mistikwok* (O. *mitig*, *mitagog*).
- C. *iskwew* 'woman' pl. *iskwewok* (O. *ikwē*, pl. *ikwēwag*).
- M. *lnu* 'human', pl. *lnuk*.
- M. *kelokokueš* 'star', pl. *kelokokueš k*.
- M. *epit* 'woman', pl. *epigik*.
- N. *mittamwossis* 'woman', pl. *mittamwossissog*.
- N. *wosketomp* 'human', pl *wosketompog*.

---

2. Concerning the dialects examined by Dawe, she says this "Inanimate nouns ending in an n change the -l inflection into an [n]. The plural marker assimilates with the /n/ of the singular form." For example kwitn 'canoe', kwitnn 'canoes' and mkîsn 'moccasin', mkîsnn 'moccasins'.
3. (A type of goose.)

[6]
- N. *manit* 'spirit, mind, soul, ghost'. pl.*manittoog* (O. *manito*, pl. *manitog*)
- N. *ahtuk* 'reindeer', pl. *ahtuhquog* (O. *atīk* pl. *atīkwag*).
- B. *atsetsi* 'glove' pl. *atsetsiks*.
- B. *pokun* 'ball'. pl. *pokuniks*.
- B. *sesenitau* 'file', pl. *sesenitaks*.
- B. *moksĭs* 'awl', pl. *moksiks*.
- Examples of the inanimate gender:
- O. *anwī* 'bullet', pl. *anwīn*.
- O. *žimāgan* 'lance', pl.*žimāganan*.
- O. *maškīki* 'medicine', pl. *maškīkiwan*.
- O. *anīt* 'fish spear', pl. *anītin*.
- O. *makak* 'box', pl. *makakon*.
- C. *tšikahikan* 'axe', pl. *tšikahikana*.
- C. *tšipayikamik* 'grave', pl. *tšipayikamikwa*.
- M. *ulidažudi* 'joy', pl. *ulidažudil*.
- M. *makamigueu* 'land', pl. *makamigal*.
- M. *m'kešen* 'shoe', pl. *m'kešenel* (O. *makisin*, pl. *makisinan*)[4]
- N. *hussun* 'stone', pl. *hussunash* (O. *asīn* is animate).
- N. *musseet* 'foot', pl. *museetash* (O. *nizīd* 'my foot', pl. *nizīdan*).
- N. *mehtug* 'tree', pl. *mehtugquash* (O. *mitig* and C. *mistik* in the sense of 'tree' are animate).
- N. *qussuk* 'rock', pl. *qussukquanash*.
- B. *autiksinatsi* 'bean', pl. *autoksinatsĭsts*.
- B. *moyĭs* 'cabin', pl. *moyĭsts*.
- B. *okhkĭn* 'bone', (that is lat. 'os'), pl. *okhkiĭsts*.
- B. *sĭnaksĭn* 'writing', pl. *sĭnaksĭsts*.

§ 6. Rules of agreement, which are of the same type as the rules that govern the genders, also apply to the plural. I mention the following: In Micmac and Natick, the attributive adjective agrees with its noun in number, but it is uninflected in Ojibway etc. The intransitive verb agrees with its subject while the transitive verb reflects the number of both the subject as well as the object. As we shall see, the pronouns also express formal distinctions in number.

---

4. But see mkĭsnn for 'moccasins' from Dawe.

Case

§ 7. Neither the contrast between nominative and accusative nor transitive or intransitive are distinguished in the noun. Nor does Algonquian have a special form for the genitive, the lack of which is supplemented by the juxtaposition of the expressions for the possessor and the possession. In general the word that indicates the possession is in the possessed form of the third person. For example, in Ojibway, for 'my father's house' one says *n-ōs o-wakaigan*, literally 'my-father-his house'. Juxtaposition without the possessive prefix is also a quite common means used to express a genitive relationship, especially when the relationship cannot actually be called possessive. We would do better then, to speak of determinative composition, since both of the joined words together express a new idea. Cases of this type in Ojibway, for example are: *iškotē-nābikwān* 'steamboat (literally 'fire-ship')', *asēma-makak* 'tobacco box', *gigō-bimidē* 'fish-oil'. How closely the parts of such a coupling or composition are mutually tied together is apparent from the fact that the first (determining) part in Ojibway frequently preserves the old stem-vowel, while this is lost in the uncompounded common singular form of the word. Examples of this are: *biwābiko-mikana* 'railway (literally 'iron-road')', *asini-wakaigan* 'house of stone (literally 'stone-house'). In Ojibway, one uses *biwābak* and *asīn* as the individual words for iron and stone.

Micmac has a peculiarity that should not go unmentioned. The nouns of this language have special forms in the singular as well as in the plural in the case in which they are tied to a negative particle. The characterizing suffix is *-inu*.

Examples:

- *mokueš lnuinu* 'not human'[5] for *lnu* 'man'.
- *mu šabuguaninu* 'not of water'; *mu šabuguaninugul* 'they contain no water',{f}[6] for *šabiguan* 'water'.

The *u* of *-inu* and the negative adjectival suffix *-tenu* mentioned later, is probably identical to the *u* we find in the negative verbal forms. May we then suspect that the negative form of the noun is a **partitive** negated by the *-u* suffix?

---

5. Perhaps even 'not one of us'
6. Perhaps 'they are not wet' or 'they have no water on them' (i).

§ 8. In Ojibway and Cree, the **vocative** singular is not as a rule, especially marked, nevertheless there are some cases in which a formal distinction between the form of address and the common word form is noticeable. In Cree *notāwi* 'my father' is usually shortened to *nota* in the vocative and *nikāwi* 'my mother' is always *neka* in the vocative. These types of contractions are much more common in Ojibway e.g., *nita* 'my brother in law', voc. *nit*; *nižišē* 'my uncle (avunculus)', voc. *nižiš*; *ningā* 'my mother', voc. *ning* (beside *ninge*). Peculiar are the vocatives *nimišo* for *nimišome* 'my uncle' (father's brother) and *nimišomis* 'my grandfather'; *nōko* for *nōkomis* 'my grandmother'. Abreviations are especially common in the vocative of proper names. Unclear are *nōse* (beside *nōs*) for *nōs* 'my father', *ningwise* (beside *ningwis*) for *ningwis* 'my son', *ninge* (beside *ning*) for *ningā* 'my mother'. Separate forms for the vocative singular are not foreign to Micmac either e.g., *nu* for *nutš* 'my father', *kidšu* for *nkitš* 'my mother'.

In the vocative plural Ojibway takes the suffix *-(i)dog*, which corresponds to *-(i)tok* in Cree. In Cree next to *-(i)tok*, *-(i)tik* is also mentioned and an alternate form of *-(i)dog* in Ojibway is *-widog*, in which *w* actually belongs to the *-wa-* stems. Preceding *-dog*, and *-tok* (*tik*) we often find the original stem vowels preserved, but *-idog* and *-itok* (*-itik*) are also suffixed to words, which are not *-i-* stems. Examples: O. *anišinābedog* for *anišinābeg* 'Indians', *anāngodog* for *anāngog* 'stars', *opīnidog* for *opīnig* 'potatoes', *kwiwizensidog* for *kwiwizensag* 'boys', *ikwēwidog* for *ikwēwag* 'women'; C. *owašišitok* (*awasisitik*) for *owašišag* (*awasisag*) 'children', *iskwetok* (*iskwetik*) for *iskwewak* 'women'. Cases of O. *-widog* in plural forms without final *w* are, for example *anišinābewidog* (beside *anišinābedog*) for *anišinābeg* 'Indians ', *ogimāwidog* (beside *ogimādog*) for *ogimāg* 'chiefs', *abinōdžiwidog* (beside *abinōdžiidog*) for *abinōdžiiag* 'children'.

Micmac has a vocative plural in *-tut*, but Natick and Blackfoot appear to lack similar forms.

§ 9. Various Algonquian languages possess a special form for the locative, which is characterized in Ojibway by *-ng*, in Cree by *-k*, and in Delaware by *-nk*. In class B. the suffix is preceded by a vowel, which is frequently identical to the plural vowel and may then be regarded as the original stem vowel, but which in other cases is different. Ojibway also has the shorter form *-g* besides *-ng*, but this is only used after words, which end with -n and the plural -n of the inanimate gender. Natick also has a locative, but this is formed by means of a -t- suffix.[7]

Examples in Ojibway:

- *nibing* for *nibi* 'water'.
- *odēnang* for *odēna* 'village' (pl. *odēnawan*).
- *nizīdang* for *nizīd* 'my foot' (pl. *nizīdan*).
- *ninindžing* for *ninindž* 'my hand' (pl. *ninindžin*).
- *kitigāning* for *kitigān* 'field' (pl. *kitigānan*). [9]
- *akikong* for *akīk* 'kettle' (pl. *akikog*).
- *nibing* for *nibin* 'summer'.
- *bibōng* for *bibōn* 'winter'.
- *o-wigiwāmiwang* for *o-wigiwāmiwan* 'their wigwams'.
- Examples in Cree:
- *maskutek* for *maskutew* 'plain'.
- *mikiwamik* for *mikiwam* 'wigwam'.
- *askikok* for *askik* 'kettle'.[8]

Examples of the -t- suffix in Natick are *neekit* and *keekit* for *neek* 'my house' and *keek* 'your (singular) house', *keekuwout* for *keekou* (your (pl) house) and *manωtat* ' basket' for *manωt*.[9]

---

7. G&B 1988 gives |-uk| as a dialectical variant. There is also a second locative present in this dialect, see footnote 9.
8. In Mi'kmaq the locative is formed with a -g.
    Examples in Micmac: mu šabuguaninug inferred from Listuguj (Restigouche) dialect mu samuqwaninug 'there is no water in place or contained there'. Mu šabuguaninugul inferred from Listuguj dialect mu samuqwaninugul 'they contain no water' (probably more like 'they are not wet' or 'they have no water on them' (i.) (Forms and emendations from Joe Wilmot).
9. In Natick there is a second locative in |-ēht^{e}ū|, |-iht^{e}ū| (the |-i| is subject to deletion, a process also called syncopation) and |-ēhkôht^{e}ū|. The difference in meaning from the ordinary locative is not certain, G&B 1988 says "Interpretation as a plural locative (apparently the usual function in Eliot) is often possible, but sometimes impossible". Examples in |-ht^{e}ū| from Eliot: *ayeuonganehtu* 'places (locative)'(1 kings 3: 2, 3), *keitotanahtu* 'cities (locative)'(Jer.44: 17), *qussukquan-uhtu* 'in the rocks (locative)'(Ps.104: 18). In the native writings this |-t^e-| is often written as |-ch-|. Examples: *nippehchu* 'water (locative)', *maitchu* 'path (locative)'. Examples in |-hkôt^{e}ū| from Eliot: *nippekontu* 'water, waters (locative)'(Ex.2: 10 and Ps. 8: 16 respectively), *ohkekontu* 'ground, earth (locative) '(Gen.2: 9, 48:12; 1 Kings 1: 23) and *wutch wosketompahtu* 'from men' (Dan. 4: 32). G&B 1988.

Subordinate forms.

§ 10. Peculiar to Algonquian are the subordinate forms of the nouns. When two third persons appear in a sentence, one is thought of as dominant and the other as subordinated. The subordinate third person is indicated by the name **obviative**. If there is still another third person in the sentence, then a further distinction is made to indicate whether he has a closer relationship to the dominant third person or to the subordinate third person. In the first case he is on the same level as the other subordinate third person, but in the second case he is further subordinated to the subordinate third person. I call this double subordinated third person **subobviative**.

For the obviative, which is only in the animate gender, Ojibway, Cree, Natick, Blackfoot, and to a certain extent also Micmac, all have distinguished forms. The subobviative that is distinguished in the animate gender, and in Ojibway sometimes, and in Cree regularly also in the inanimate gender, is lacking in Micmac, Natick and Blackfoot.

In Ojibway and Cree, the transitive verbal forms vary according to the third person object, depending on whether the object is independent, obviative or subobviative, while the obviative is also reflected in the verbs of Blackfoot.

§ 11. The **obviative**, which is the same for both numbers, is formed by the addition of an -*n* suffix to the word stem in Ojibway. This -*n* is thus, also in class B words, preceded by the same vocalism as the -*g* of the plural. In Cree the -*n* suffix has been lost and only the preceding -*a* or -*wa* has been retained. This uniform vocalism form must be considered in the same manner as the vocalization of the plural. The actual sign for the obviative has also been lost in Natick and the thematic -*oh*, -*uh*, and -*ah* appear to be the characteristic of this form. Micmac on the other hand has kept an -*l* (-*el*) obviative suffix, which corresponds to the O. -*n* (suffix). The formation of the obviative is not completely clear in Blackfoot. As has already been stated in the preceding paragraph, the obviative belongs exclusively to the animate gender.

Examples in Ojibway:

- *anišinaben* for *anišinabe* 'Indian'.
- *maniton* for *manito* 'spirit'.
- *nōsan* for *nōs* 'my father'.

- *ningaian* for *ninga* 'my mother'.
- *amikwan* for *amik* 'beaver'.
- *opinin* for *opin* 'potato'.
- *anangon* for *anang* 'star'.

Examples in Cree:
- *owašiša* (*awasisa*) for *owašiš* (*awasis*) 'child'.
- *mistikwa* for *mistik* 'tree'.
- Example in Micmac:
- *utšel* 'his father', cf. *nutš* 'my father', *kutš* 'your (singular) father'.
- Example in Natick:
- *anogqsoh* for *anogqs* 'star'.
- Examples in Blackfoot:
- *ninnaii* for *ninnau* 'man'.
- *ponokŏmitaii* for *ponokŏmita* 'horse'.

In Ojibway, the **subobviative** of both numbers is derived from the obviative. In certain cases it is formed by suffixing *-ini*, and in others by changing the termination to *-ini* (for a limited class of personal names to *-ani*). The specific rules may be omitted here. It must also be mentioned however that a number of words use *-inawan* as an alternate form for *-ini*.

While the subobviative is generally only for words of animate gender in Ojibway, Cree has separate subobviative forms for the singular of animate and inanimate words. For the animate gender, the subobviative singular, and plural are derived from the common singular form, by adding the suffix *-iliwa* (*-iyiwa*). However the inanimate gender forms the subobviative by attaching the suffixes *-iliw* (*-iyiw*) for the singular and *-iliwa* (*-iyiwa*) for the plural, to the common word form. [11]

Examples in Ojibway:

- *manitonini* for *manito* 'spirit', obv. *maniton*.
- *nisīminini* for *nisīm* 'my daughter-in-law', obv. *nisīmin*.
- *ogwisini*(*wan*) for *ogwisan* 'his son'.
- *ikwēwini* for *ikwē* 'woman', obv. *ikwēwan*.
- *wiwini* for *wiwan* 'his wife'.
- *ogini* (*wan*) for *ogin* 'his mother'.
- Examples in Cree:
- *okosisiliwa* (singular, plural) cf. *okosisa* 'his son'
- *o-masinahikaniliw* sing., *o-masinahikaniliwa* plur., cf. *o-masinahikana* 'his book', *masimahikan* 'book'.

Possessive inflection

§ 12. The possessive prefixes are for the most part the same as the pronominal prefixes in the conjugations and partially the same as the individual personal pronouns. Similar to those, the possessive and the verbal inflections distinguish between an exclusive and an inclusive first person plural. The pluralization of the elements, which indicate possessor are further suffixed to suffixes, which in many cases, (although not always) are vocalized as the original word stem so that we can often times (especially in Ojibway) learn the actual vowel stem from the possessive forms. The plural formation of the nouns, which are provided with the possessive prefixes, differ according to the gender. It can also be noticed -except in Blackfoot- in animate words, a noun, which has the prefix of the third person in front of it, is always in the obviative.

Often times the possessive inflection in Ojibway and Cree is extended by affixing an -m to the word stem. The function of this affix seems to be to emphasize the concept of property. Examples: O. *nind-ogimām* 'my own chief': *nind-ogimā* 'my chief', *od-ogimāman* 'his own chief': *od-ogimān* 'his chief', *nind-akīm* 'my own piece of land': *nind-akī* 'my land', *od-ažaweškom* 'his own sword'': *od-ažawešk* 'his sword'; C. *ni-pižiskim* 'my own animal'; *ni-pižiskiw* 'my animal', *ni-mistikom* 'my own tree': *ni-mistik* 'my tree', *o-mistikoma* 'his own tree': *o-mistikwa* 'his tree', *ni-waskahikanim* 'my own house': *ni-waskahikan* 'my house'.

This -m suffix is also found in Blackfoot but it appears that it is not used as often in this language. Nevertheless it is clear from examples like *nĭt-ake-m* 'my younger sister (literally the woman belonging to me)' and *tsanetsima kĭt-stuyi-m-ists* 'how many are your winters (that is, how old are you?)' that it does exist in this language.

The names of body parts and kinship terms always have a prefix in most Algonquian languages. Some other words in certain dialects also cannot be used without a prefix. If one wishes to use body parts or some other words in an absolute state and not in relation to a certain person, then various languages use an abstract prefix, which is *mi-* in Cree and *m+* vowel in Natick and Blackfoot. Examples of words that do not appear without a prefix: O. *nōs* 'my father', *kōs* 'your (singular) father', *ningā* 'my mother', *ogin* 'his mother', *ništigwān* 'my head', *nizīd* 'my foot', *nindē* 'my heart', *nibīd* 'my tooth', *wibīd* 'his tooth', C. *notāwi* 'my father', *kotāwi* 'your (singular) father', *mistikwān* '(the) head', *nistikwān* 'my head', *miwat* 'medicine pouch', *niwat* 'my medicine pouch', *wiwat* 'his medicine pouch', M. *nutš* 'my father', *kutš* 'your (sing.) father', *nkitš* 'my mother', N. *nωsh* 'my father', *kωsh* 'your (sing.) father', *nωkas* 'my mother', *meepit* 'tooth', *neepit* 'my tooth', *weebit* 'his tooth', *menutcheg* 'hand', *wennutcheg* 'his hand', *mehtauog* 'ear', *kehtauog* 'your (sing.) ear', *musseet* 'foot', *nusseet* 'my foot' *muhkont* 'leg', *wuhkont* 'his leg'. B. *nĭna* 'my father', *kĭna* 'your (sing.) father', *unni* 'his father', *maåks* 'grandfather/mother', *naåks* 'my grandfather/mother', *motsĭs* 'hand', *notsĭs* 'my hand'.

I will not discuss here the irregularities that occur in the possessive inflections, since they certainly cannot be cleared up except by a complete comparison of all related languages, for which I do not have the required material.

§ 13. In this paragraph, I will give an overview of the affixes that characterize the possessive inflections except for the *-m* suffix that I have already treated.

First person singular.

- 'my': O. *nin(d)* ,*-nidž*, *ni-*, *n-*, M. *n-*, N. *n+* vowel, B. *nit(s)-*, *no-*, *ni-*, *n-*.
- 'my' (plural): with these prefixes as well, but for the animate gender with the suffix O. *-g* (after the stem-vowel) C. *-(a)k*, *-(wo)k*, M. *-k*, N. *-(o)g*, *-(wo)g*[10], B. *-(i)ks*, and with the inanimate gender the suffix O. *-n* (after the stem vowel), C. *-(a)*, *-(wa)*, M. *-(e)l*, N. *-(a)(na)sh*, B. *-(ĭ)sts*.

Second person singular.

- 'your': O. *ki(d)-*, *kidž-*, *k-*, C. *ki(t)-*, *k-*, M. *k-*, N. *k+* vowel, *k-*, B. *kit(s)-*, *ko-*, *ki-*, *k-*.
- 'your' (plural): with these same prefixes, but with the suffixes —for the two varying genders—, which are mentioned under 'my' (plural object).

---

10. Some words have a dialectical variant of this ending in *-unk*.

Third person singular:

- 'his'; O. o(d)-, widž-, w-, −(ōsan, ōkomisan), C. o (+)-, w-, −(otāwia, okoma), M. u-, −(utsel), N. w+ vowel, w-, B. ot(s)-, o-. Apart from Blackfoot, the rule as it applies to the languages we are dealing with here is that when an animate noun takes a third person prefix, it stands in the obviative.
- 'his' (plural): with these same prefixes, but with the addition of the suffixes that correspond to the genders, mentioned under 'my' (plural). In Micmac and Blackfoot pluralization of the noun for the animate gender also takes place in this case by means of the suffixes that correspond to this gender. Micmac also lacks the obviative suffix in this case.

Exclusive first person plural.

- 'our': with the prefix of the first person singular, but adding the following suffixes to the word-stem: O. C. -nān, N. -nun, -un,[11] B. -nan. Micmac has the suffix -nen for the animate gender and -nel for the inanimate gender. Where we find -nen given for a word of inanimate gender we must assume it is an error.
- 'our' (plural): Apart from Micmac, the suffix is the same as for the singular exclusive 'our' but with the additional suffixes O. -ig, C. -ak, B. -iks for the animate gender and O, -in, C. -a, B. -ĭsts for the inanimate gender. In Natick the previously mentioned suffix -nun has been extended to -nunnonut.[12] In Micmac we find a prefix, which is the same as the singular exclusive 'our', but the combination of the suffixes becomes -nak in place of *-nen-ak for words of animate gender and -nual in place of *-nel-al for words of inanimate gender. Next to -nual however the form -nen is also given, but this is probably due to an error.

---

11. The Natick suffix is actually -(n)un(on) or (-unôn). The last syllable, (on) or (ôn) deletes word finally, but is retained before additional endings.
12. This is the locative ending. G&B 1988 gives -(n)unnonash for the pl. ending) in the plural form of the inanimate noun and -(n)un becomes -(n)unnonog in the plural of the animate noun.

Inclusive first person plural.

- 'our': takes the prefix of the second person singular, but affixing the following suffixes to the word stem: O. *-nān*, C. *-now*, M. *-nu*, B. *-nun*. Concerning Natick, I am uncertain.[13]
- 'our' (plural): Apart from Micmac, the form of the singular inclusive 'our' is used, but with further affixing of the suffixes - differing for the two genders -, which have been mentioned under exclusive 'our' (plural) (in Cree *-now-ak* becomes *-now-ok*). Concerning Natick I am not sufficiently informed. In Micmac the prefix is the same as the singular inclusive 'our', but the combination of the suffixes become *-nak* in place of *-nu-ak* for words of animate gender (I can give no definite answer concerning the inanimate gender: Presumably the compound suffix would be *-nu-al*, which would correspond to the exclusive form).

Second person plural.

- 'your' (plural): takes the prefix of the second person singular, but with addition of the following suffixes to the word stem O. *-wa*, C. *-waw*, M. *-uau*, N. *-ou*, *-eu*, *-ω*, *-nω*, B. *-oau*.[14]
- 'your' (plural: with plural noun): Apart from Micmac the inflection is the same as for 'your' (plural: with singular noun), but with the addition of the suffixes O. *-g*, C. *-ak* (*-ok*),[15] B. *-iks* for the animate gender and O. *-n*, C. *-a*, N. *-wout*,[16] B. *-ists* for the inanimate gender. In Micmac, where the prefix is also the same as for the singular noun, the combination of the suffixes becomes *-uak*, *-ual* in place of *-uau-ak*, *-uau-al*. The distribution of the combined suffixes amongst both genders, do not appear to correspond completely with what we might expect.

---

13. Again, the Natick suffix is actually *-(n)un(on)* or (*-unôn*). The last syllable, (*on*) or (*ôn*) deletes word finally, but is retained before additional endings.
14. The Natick suffix is actually *-(n)ω(oh)* or (*-uwôw*). The last syllable, (*oh*) or (*ôw*) deletes word finally, but is retained before additional endings.
15. The N. suffix here is the previous (*-uwôw*) with the addition of *-g* as in *-uog* (e.g., *kunnashanittoomuog* 'your (pl.) spirits') with *-m* or (*-um*) forming possessed themes cf. §12. See G&B 1988).
16. This is the locative ending and the corresponding plural is in *-woash*, See G&B 1988 (e.g., *kummatcheseonganωwoash* 'your (pl.) sins').

Third person plural.

- 'their': takes the third person singular prefix, but adds the suffixes O. -*wa-n*, C. -*wa*, M. -*ual*, B. -*oaiau* for the animate gender and O. -*wa*, C. -*waw*, M. -*ual*, N. -*ou*, -*no*, B. -*oaiau* for the inanimate gender. I am not able to give the suffix for the animate gender in Natick with any degree of certainty.[17] Besides the -*wa* ending of the animate gender Cree has the by-form -*waw-a*, which appears to be the suffix of the inanimate gender combined with the -*a* suffix of the obviative. The O. -*wa-n* suffix also differs from the inanimate -*wa* only by the presence of the obviative suffix.
- 'their' (plural noun): just as the 'their' (singular noun), but with the addition of the suffixes O. -*n*, C. -*a*, N. -*wout*,[18] B. -*ists* (Micmac has no similar suffix) for the inanimate gender. For the animate gender, most of the dialects have exactly the same form as for the 'their'(singular noun)', it should be noted however, that Cree always has -*wawa* for the 'their' (plural noun) and Micmac sometimes has the form -*uakal*, which shows plural characterization, besides the form -*ual*.[19] In Blackfoot, the animate form for 'their' (plural noun) always takes the plural suffix -*iks*.

[15]

§ 14. It cannot yet be determined in all cases how the equivalent prefixes correspond within the same dialect or between different tongues. What for example is the relationship of O. *nidž-* and *kidž-* to B. *nĭt(s)-* and *kĭt(s)-*? An O.*odž*, which should correspond with B. *ot(s)-* is not found, but instead one finds *widž-* no less dim is the relation of O. *nidž, kidž, widž* to *ni(n)(d)-, ki(d)-, o(d)-* and of B. *nĭt(s)-, kĭt(s)- ot(s)-* to *ni-(no-), ki- (ko-), o-*. In the possessive inflection B. *nĭt(s)-, kĭt(s)*, and *ot(s)-* function as pre-vowel forms, but in the conjugation of the verb one finds such forms as *nit-, kit-,* and *ot-* whose relationship to *ni-, ki-* and *o-* is the same as in Cree or as that of O. *nind-, kid-,* and -*od* to *nin-, ki-,* and *o-*. Concerning the shortest form of the prefixes (*n-,k-,w-*), it is quite probable that these are at the same time the oldest since the prefixed pronouns are the most reduced, which would have required a long time. Where the prefixed pronouns are not mutilated or are only a little, they will

---

17. Again, the Natick suffix is actually -*(n)ω(oh)* or *(-uwôw)*. The last syllable, *(oh)* or *(ôw)* deletes word finally, but is retained before additional endings).
18. This is the locative ending and the corresponding plural is in -*woash* See G&B 1988).
19. The Natick suffix is the same as for 'their' singular noun.

eventually however become non-syllabic prefixes. However, based on a comparison of the Algonquian languages it is certain that this had already taken place in the period of unity. Also decidedly old, as just mentioned, is the juxtaposition of forms with a final dental before initial vowels and forms without a final dental before initial consonants. A phenomenon that is also worthy of our attention is the real or apparent absence of the third-person-prefix in some words, which begin with *o-*: we can ask the question whether the prefix *o-* has been contracted here with the initial vowel.

Judging the suffixes and the preceding vowels also provides some difficulties. What for example is the reason that words such as O. *mokomān* 'knife' pl. *mokomānan* exhibit *i* and not *a* for the suffixes that pluralize the possessor. And concerning the suffixes themselves we are surprised among other things, by the contrast between O. *-ig* and C. *-ak* for the pluralization of the animate nouns for 'our' (plural noun). Unusual are the plural forms of Natick in *-nonut* and *-wout*,[20] which remind us of the locative through their termination in *-ut*: cf. *nunnutcheganunnonut* ' our hands', *kenutcheganωwout* 'your (plural) hands', *wunnutcheganωwout* 'their hands' with *neekunonut* 'in our house', *keekuwout* 'in your (plural) house' *weekuwout* or *wekuwomut* 'in his house'.[21] In Micmac we even find some forms, which inspire our suspicions and require urgent verification. For the moment I must limit myself to pointing out problems, in the hope that they will be resolved by a comparison of a larger body of material.

§ 15. For further clarification a few paradigms follow. O. *akīk*, C. *askik* 'kettle'; O. *nōs*, M. *nutš*, N. *nωsh* 'my father'; N. *nunnaumon* 'my son'; B. *pun* 'bracelet', may serve as examples for the animate gender.

Singular of the noun

		O.	C.
1	sing.	nind-akīk	niti-askik

---

20. These are the locative endings and the corresponding plurals are in *-(n)onash* and *-woash*, See G&B 1988.
21. Again, all of these final *-ut* endings are locatives and would be in *-ash* in the plural.

	O.	C.
2 sing.	ki-akīk	kit-askik
3 sing.	od-akikon	ot-askikwa
1 pl. e.	nind-akikonān	kit-askikonān
1 pl. i.	kid-akikonān	kit-askikonow
2 pl.	kid-akikowa	kit-askikowaw
3 pl.	od-akikowan	ot-askikowa(wa)

Plural of the noun

	O.	C.
1 sing.	nind-akikog	nit-askikwok
2 sing.	kid-akikog	kit-askikwok
3 sing.	od-akikon	ot-askikwa
1 pl. e.	nind-akikonānig	nit-askikonānak
1 pl. i.	kid-akikonānig	kit-askonowok
2 pl.	kid-akikowag	kit-askikowawok
3 pl.	od-akikowan	ot-askikowawa

Singular of the noun

	O.	M.	N.
1 sing.	nōs	nu(t)š	nωsh
2 sing.	kōs	ku(t)š	kωsh
3 sing.	ōsan	u(t)šel	ωshoh
1 pl. e.	nōsinān	nu(t)šinen	nωshun
1 pl. i.	kōsinān	ku(t)šinu	kωshun†
2 pl.	kōsiwa	ku(t)šinau	kωsheu (kωshω)

† J.S.

		O.	M.	N.
3	pl.	ōsiwan	u(t)šiual	(ω or i)sh(ωoh or ioh)†

Plural of the noun [17]

		O.	M.	N.
1	sing.	nōsag	nu(t)šak?†	nωshog†
2	sing.	kōsag	ku(t)šak?†	kωshog†
3	sing.	ōsan	u(t)šel?†	ωshoh†
1	pl. e.	nōsinānig	nu(t)šinak	nωshunonog†
1	pl. i.	kōsinānig	ku(t)šinak	kωshunonog†
2	pl.	kōsiwag	ku(t)šiuak	kωshωoog†
3	pl.	ōsiwan	u(t)šiuakal	(ω or i) sh (ωoh or ioh)†

N.

		Singular of the noun	Plural of the noun
1	sing.	nunnaumon	nunnaumonog
2	sing.	kenaumon	kenaumonog†
3	sing.	wunnaumonuh	wunnaumonuh†
1	pl. e.	nunnaumonun†	nunnaumonunonog†
1	pl. i.	kenaumonun†	kenaumonunonog†
2	pl.	kenaumonω†	kenaumonωoog†
3	pl.	wunnaumon(ωuh or iyeuoh)†	wunnaumon(ωuh or iyeuoh)†

† J.S.

B.

		Singular of the noun	Plural of the noun
1	sing.	*no-pun*	*no-puniks*
2	sing.	*ko-pun*	*ko-puniks*
3	sing.	*o-pun*	*o-puniks*
1	pl. e.	*no-punĭnan*	*no-punĭnaniks*
1	pl. i.	*ko-punĭnun*	*ko-punĭnuniks*
2	pl.	*ko-punoau*	*ko-punoauiks*
3	pl.	*o-punoaiau*	*o-punoaiauiks*

§ 16. As examples of the inanimate gender I choose: O. *mokomān*, C. *mokumān* 'knife'; M. *nāye* 'my thing', M. *ntokuan* 'my dress'; N. *metah* 'heart'; N. *neek* 'my house'; N. *menutcheg* 'hand'; B. *sĭnaksĭn* 'writing'.

Singular of the noun

		O.	C.
1	sing.	*nin-mokomān*	*ni-mokumān*
2	sing.	*ki-mokomān*	*ki-mokumān*
3	sing.	*o-mokomān*	*o-mokumān*
1	pl. e.	*nin-mokomāninān*	*nin-mokumāninān*
1	pl. i.	*ki-mokomāninān*	*ki-mokumāninow*
2	pl.	*ki-mokomāniwa*	*ki-mokumāniwaw*
3	pl.	*o-mokomāniwa*	*o-mokumāniwaw*

Plural of the noun

		O.	C.
1	sing.	nin-mokomānan	ni-mokumāna
2	sing.	ki-mokomānan	ki-mokumāna
3	sing.	o-mokomānan	o-mokumāna
1	pl. e.	nin-mokomāninānin	nin-mokumānināna
1	pl. i.	ki-mokomāninānin	ki-mokumāninowa
2	pl.	ki-mokomāniwan	ki-mokumāniwawa
3	pl.	o-mokomāniwan	o-mokumāniwawa

M.
Singular of the noun

1	sing.	nāye	ntokuan
2	sing.	kāye	ktokuan
3	sing.	uāye	uftokuan
1	pl. e.	nāynen (!?)	ntokuannel
1	pl. i.	kāynu	
2	pl.	kāyuau	ktokuanuau
3	pl.	uāyual	uftokuanual

Plural of the noun

1	sing.		ntokuanel
2	sing.		ktokuanel
3	sing.		uftokuanel

1	pl. e.	nāynen (!?)	ntokuannual
1	pl. i.		
2	pl.	kāyuau (!?)	ktokuanual
3	pl.	uāyual	uftokuanual

N.

Singular of the noun

1	sing.	nuttah	neek
2	sing.	kuttah	keek
3	sing.	wuttah	week
1	pl. e.	nuttahhun	neekun
1	pl. i.	kuttahhun†	keekun†
2	pl.	kuttahhou	keekou
3	pl.	wuttahhou	weekou

N.

		Singular of the noun	Plural of the noun
1	sing.	nunnutcheg	nunnutcheganash
2	sing.	kenutcheg	kenutchega(na)sh
3	sing.	wunnutcheg	wunnutchega(na)sh
1	pl. e.	nunnutcheganun	nunnutcheganunnonut nunnutcheganunnonash†
1	pl. i.	kunnutcheganun†	kunnutcheganunnonash†
2	pl.	kenutcheganω	kenutcheganωwout kenutcheganωwoash†

† J.S.

		Singular of the noun	Plural of the noun
3	pl.	wunnutcheganω	wunnutcheganωwout wunnutcheganωwoash†

B.

		Singular of the noun	Plural of the noun
1	sing.	ni-sĭnaksĭn	ni-sĭnaksĭn
2	sing.	ki-sĭnaksĭn	ki-sĭnaksĭn
3	sing.	o-sĭnaksĭn	o-sĭnaksĭn
1	pl. e.	ni-sĭnaksĭnan	ni-sĭnaksĭnanĭsts
1	pl. i.	ki-sĭnaksĭnun	ki-sĭnaksĭnunĭsts
2	pl.	ki-sĭnaksĭnoau	ki-sĭnaksĭnoauĭsts
3	pl.	o-sĭnaksĭnoaiau	o-sĭnaksĭnoaiauĭsts

M.²²

		Animate noun		Inanimate Noun	
		Singular of the noun	Plural of the noun	Singular of the noun	Plural of the noun
1	sing.	ntus	ntusk	ntul	ntull

---

22. Because of what appear to be a number of troublesome areas in the Micmac forms given above, the possessive inflections are given below from Dawe. There does seem to be agreement in the endings of the plural exclusive and inclusive endings of Cree for the singular of the noun and Dawe uses this to postulate different endings for these forms in Proto-Algonquian than those put forth by Bloomfield corresponding to the Ojibway forms given above. She also reports that one of her sources mentions a distinction between these forms in Arapaho as well, but says that the distinction was only mentioned and not given. Many authors have compared these nominal inflections with the so called -n endings of the indicative in verbal categories (see G&B 1988 for the full -n, -m and -w endings for Massachusett), but Goddard warns against drawing an erroneous etymological connection here (see Goddard 1983 and 2007). Still the similarities may

† J.S.

		Animate noun		Inanimate Noun	
		Singular of the noun	Plural of the noun	Singular of the noun	Plural of the noun
2	sing.	ktus	ktusk	ktul	ktull
3	sing.	wtusl	wtus	wtul	wtull
1	pl. e.	ntusinen	ntusinaq	ntulinen	ntulinal
1	pl. i.	ktusinu	ktusinaq	ktulinu	ktulinal
2	pl.	ktusiwow	ktuswaq	ktulwow	ktulwal
3	pl.	wtuswal	wtuswa	wtulwow	wtulwal[†]

Temporal inflections

§ 17. Preterite forms are derived from the possessive forms by the means of -*ban*. The same -*ban* is a suffix of the past tense in the conjugation.[23] Examples of the preterite in nouns: O. *nōsiban* 'my deceased father', *kōkomisinaban* 'our (incl.) deceased grandmother', *nind-ogimāmiban* 'my previous or deceased chief', *nind-akikoban* 'my previous kettle, which I had', *ki-wakaiganiwaban* 'your (plural) previous house', C. *ni-musomiban* 'my deceased grandfather', *ni-mokumāniban* 'my previous knife'. One can also derive such -*ban*- forms from the absolute use of substantives -mostly proper nouns. This distinction in Ojibway is quite closely related to the actual Algonkin *Zabieban* 'the deceased Xavier'. If, in Ojibway and actual Algonkin, deceased people one has not known are spoken of, it is not uncommon for -*go-ban* to be used instead of -*ban* so that O. *kokimisinagoban* has the meaning of 'our (incl.) deceased grandmother whom we have not known.' This traditional preterite of the noun is based on the same psychic inclination, as the dubiative or the traditional conjugation of the verb.

---

prove helpful to the advanced student as a tool to memorize both sets of patterns. Daughter is used here for the animate noun and boat is used for the inanimate noun.

23. This phenomenon is frequently referred to as absentative in the contemporary literature.

† J.S.

Micmac has suffixes, which have an equivalent meaning as -*ban* when affixed to the nouns, although they are not etymologically related. These suffixes are used for absolute nouns as well as being affixed to possessive forms. For the animate gender one uses -*ak* for the singular, -*ok* for proper nouns, -(*k*)*ik* for the plural. For the inanimate gender -*ek* is the singular and -*kel* or -*gel* is the plural suffix. Examples: *lnuak*, pl. *lnkik*, beside *lnu* for man; human; *epitak*, pl. *epitkik*, beside *epit* 'woman'; *nu(t)šak* beside *nu(t)š* 'my father'; *nu(t)šinakik* beside *nu(t)šinak*, and *ku(t)šinak* 'our fathers'; *Luiok* beside *Lui* 'Louis'; *pibenakanek*, pl. *pibenakankel*, beside *pibenakan* 'bread'. There are also words, which prefix *še-ben* or *šen* to the common preterite suffixes. Both of these elements -just as -*ek* — also fulfill a role in the conjugation. In *še-ben* we may probably see a compound of -*ben* = O. C. -*ban* (cf. § 47).[24]

If one wishes to give a future meaning to nouns in Algonquian, it can be accomplished simply by means of denominative verbal forms.

Noun-forming suffixes

§ 18. The formation of the noun in Algonquian is almost exclusively by means of suffixing and most of the languages that belong to this family actually completely lack proper noun forming prefixes. In Blackfoot, such prefixes play a somewhat important role, although they always appear simultaneously with completing suffixes. I limit myself to mentioning a few simple suffixes. I wish first however, only to point out that compounds appearing in the second part of the composition such as O. *gami*, C. -*kami* 'water', O. -*nag* 'canoe'. [21] O. -*wigwamig*, C. *wikamik* 'house'. O. -(*w*)*ābo*, C. -*āpo* 'liquid' etc. are not actually suffixes and belong to the realm of lexicology rather than to that of grammar.

---

24. In Natick the nominal preterite is |-ī| for the singular of both genders, and |-uk| for the animate plural with the obviative in |-uk| or |-ukoh|. Examples of the singular: a. *numissoomissi* 'my late grandfather', *nooshi* 'my late father' i. *wuttiheummoi* 'his former property'. Eamples of the animate plural: *nussontimmom̠i̠n̠n̠a̠nuk* (the underlined vowels here have various attested alternative vowels) 'our (excl.) late chiefs', *kooshinnanuk* 'our (incl.) late fathers'. Obviative: *oohkassuk* 'her late mother', *wunnechannussukkoh* 'his deceased children'. G&B 1988 also says this "Stems and plural-possessor markers that drop the final syllable in the singular have an absentative singular without |-ī| but with the final syllable retained: *nwshinnon* 'our (excl.) late father'", *nuttahkennan* 'our (excl.) former land'.

Diminutives are formed with O. *-ns*, C. *-s (-š)*, *sis (šiš)*, M. *-(t)ši(t)š (-džitš)*, N. *-es, -emes*. Both of these Natick suffixes are respectively 'small' and 'least'. In class *B*. a vowel also precedes O. *-ns* and C. *-s(-š)*, which in certain cases, is the old stem vowel. In Cree diminutives of diminutives are not uncommon and the suffix *-kiš* gives the diminutive a pejorative meaning. Concerning the mutual relationship of the aforementioned suffixes C. *-sis (šiš)* corresponds to the Micmac suffix and C. *s. (-š)* is identical to the N. *-es*. C. *-s (-š)* also corresponds to O. *-š (-iš, -oš, -wiš)* although these do not possess a diminutive force but rather a pejorative one. O. *-ns* appears to stand alone unless we can make a connection with N. *-emes*. O.*-ns* and N.*-emes* are probably compound suffixes. In Ojibway one finds *-s* — not *-ns* with preceeding vowel — for the diminutive suffix of words, which end in the short syllable *-gan*, but giving the impression that in this case *-gans* originated from*-ganens* (cf. the words in *-gān* whose diminutive ends in *-gānens*).

Examples of the diminutive in Ojibway:

- *ogimāns* for *ogimā* 'chief', pl. *ogimāg*.
- *oškinawens* for *oškinawe* 'young man' pl. *oškinaweg*.
- *kokōšens* 'piglet' for *kokōš* 'pig', pl. *kokōšag*.
- *kitigānens* 'garden' for *kitigān* 'field', pl. *kitigānan*.
- *opwāgans* for *opwāgan* 'pipe', pl. *opwāganag*.
- *pakaakwens* 'chick' for *pakaakwē* 'hen', pl. *pakaakwēiag*.
- *pižikins* 'calf' for *pižiki* 'cow', pl. *pižikiwag*.
- *asīnins* for *asīn* 'stone', pl. *asīnig*.
- *anītins* for *anīt* 'spear', pl. *anītin*.
- *anāngons* for *anāng* 'star', pl. *anāngog*.
- *makakons* for *makak* 'box', pl. *makakon*.
- Examples of the pejorative in Ojibway:
- *kwiwizensiš* for *kwiwizens* 'boy' pl. *kwiwizensag*.
- *mokomāniš* for *mokomān* 'knife', pl. *mokomānan*.
- *abinōdžiiš* for *abinōdži* 'child', pl. *abinōdžiiag*.
- *asīniš* for *asīn* 'stone', pl. *asīnig*.
- *anītiš* for *anīt* 'spear', pl. *anītin*.
- *mitigoš* for *mitig* 'tree', pl. *mitigog*.
- *wāwanoš* for *wāwan* 'egg', pl. *wāwanon*.
- *ogimāwiš* for *ogimā* 'chief', pl. *ogimāg*.
- *ininiwiš* for *inini* 'man', pl. *ininiwag*.
- *sibiwiš* for *sibi* 'river', pl. *sibiwan*.

- *odēnawiš* for *odēna* 'village', pl. *odēnawan*.
- Examples of the diminutive in Cree, formed with *-s* (*-š*):
- *meskanās* for *meskanaw* 'road'.
- *masinahiganis* for *masinahigan* 'book'.
- *astisis* for *astis* 'mitten'.
- *mustusus* 'calf' for *mustus* 'cow'.
- *mistikus* for *mistik* 'tree'.

Examples of the diminutive in Natick:

- *nunkompaes, nunkompaemes* for *nunkomp* 'young man', pl. *nunkompaog*.
- *nunksquaes, nunksquaemes* for *nunksqau* 'damsel', pl. *nunksqauog*.
- *mehtugquemes* for *mehtug* 'tree', pl. *mehtugquash*,
- Examples of the diminutive in Cree, formed with *-sis* (*-šiš*):
- *nabesis* (*napešiš*) 'boy' for *nabew* (*napew*) 'man'.
- *iskwesis* (*iskwešiš*) 'girl' for *iskwew* 'woman'.
- Examples of the diminutive in Micmac:
- *albadudžitš* for *albadu* 'boy'.
- *Mišel(t)ši(t)š* for *mišel* 'Michel'.[25]
- *wigwom(t)ši(t)š* for *wigwom* 'wigwam'.

Examples of double diminutive words in Cree:

- *nābesisis* (*nāpešišiš*) for *nābesis* (*nāpešiš*) 'boy'.
- *nābew* (*nāpew*) 'man'.
- *mistikusis* for *mistikus* 'small tree' *mistik* 'tree'.
- Examples of the pejorative in Cree:
- *nāpešiškiš, nāpešišiškiš* for *nāpešiš* 'boy': *nāpew* 'man'.
- *tšimāniškiš* for *tšimāniš* 'small canoe': *tšimān* 'canoe'.

§ 19. I have put aside other denominitive suffixes, as they are considered less important from a morphological point of view. Rather, I deem it necessary to make mention of some quite customary deverbal suffixes.

Verbal-abstracts are formed by *-win* in Ojibway and Cree. In both languages one finds such verbal abstracts not only for the active but also for the passive verbs.

Examples in Ojibway:

- *ožibiigewin* 'writing' for *ožibiige* 'he writes'.

---

25. A man's name in French.

- *dibaamāgewin* 'payment (from the stand point of the one paying) ',
- *dibaamāgowin* 'payment (from the stand point of him, who is being paid)', cf.
- *dibaamāge* 'he pays', *nin-dibaamāgo* 'I receive payment'.
- *dibākonigewin* 'judgment (from the stand point of the one who judges)',
- *dibākonigowin* 'judgment (from the stand point of the one who is being judged)', cf. *dibākonige* 'he judges', *nin-dibākonigo* 'I am being judged'.
- *migādiwin* 'fight' for *migādiwag* 'they fight with each other'.
- *ganōnidiwin* 'conversation' for *ganōnidiwag* 'they speak with each other'.
- *dōdamowin* 'deed' for *dōdam* 'he does', *dōdamog* 'they do'.
- *minikwesiwin* 'non-drinking' for (*kawin*) *minikwesi* 'he does not drink'.

Examples in Cree:

- *masinahikewin* 'writing' for *masinahikew* 'he writes'.
- *sākihiwewin* 'love (for someone)' for *sākihiwew* 'he loves'.
- *sākitāwin* 'love' for *sākitaw* 'he loves it' (inanimate object).
- *ni-sākihikawiwin* 'my being loved', cf. *ni-sākihikawin* 'One who loves me'.
- *ni-miweyimikowin* 'my being respected'. cf. *ni-miweyimik* 'he respects me'.
- *ayamihāwin* 'prayer' for *ayamihaw* 'he prays'.
- *pikiskwewin* 'speech' for *pikiskwew* 'he speaks'.
- *miyosiwin* 'beauty (of someone)' for *miyosiw* 'he is pretty'.
- *mayātanowin* 'ugliness (of something)' for *mayātan* 'that is ugly'.
- *kižitewin* 'warmth' for *kižitew* 'it is warm'.

Regarding Micmac and Natick, I am not sufficiently informed.[26,27]
Concerning Blackfoot, *-sĭnni* and *-ani* are suffixes with which verbal-abstracts are formed.

Examples:

- *kŏmossĭnni* 'the theft' for *kŏmosiu* 'he steals'.
- *amĭssosĭnni* 'rise' for *amĭsso* 'he rises'.[28]
- *puksipusĭnni* 'arrival' for *puksipu* 'he comes here'.
- *pisĭnni* 'entrance' for *ai-pim* 'he enters' (*ai* is prefix).
- *mŭksĭnasĭnni* 'badness' for *mŭksĭnŭm* 'he is bad'.
- *ketani* 'baking' for *ketau* 'he bakes'.

Person-indicating nouns with passive meanings are derived from verbs in Ojibway and Cree by means of the suffix *-gan*.

Examples in Ojibway:

- *nind-inawemāgan* 'my relative' for *nind-inawema* 'I am related to him'.
- *nin-widžiwāgan* 'my companion' for *nin-widžiwa* 'I accompany him'.

---

26. In Micmac many verbs can "form nouns by changing *-i* into *-uti* or *-waqn*, with contraction of the first syllable, if the verb is susceptible to it." (see appendix on secondary verbs) Examples: *Wisqîsi, sin, sit* (these forms are taken from H&F 1990 where the given form represents the first person e.g., 'I am sick' and the forms in *sin* and *sit* represent the second and third person inflections respectively. This type of notation helps show whether the third person of the verb terminates in the *t* or the *k, g, q* sound) 'to be sick'; *wisqîsuti* and *wisqîsuaqn* 'contagious disease'; *welita'si, sin, sit* 'to be content, happy'; *wlita'suti, wlita'suaqn* 'happiness, joy'; *sape'wi, win, wit* 'to be wise, holy, virtuous'; *sape'wuti* 'virtue, wisdom'; *elue'wi, win, wit* 'to be bad, a sinner'; *elue'wuti: weskijinui, uin, uit* 'to be born, to live'; *wskijinuuti* 'birth, life, nature' See H&F 1990.
27. In Natick "|-ēnunū-|, forms agent nouns from AI stems and TI themes" Examples: AI *wawawenin* 'wittness' from *wawá* 'to act as a witness' from *waw* 'to know', "*nananoowaenin* 'justice of the peace' from the stem in *nanauwunnuacheg* 'magistrates'", "*negonshaenin* 'ruler'" (is there a possible etymology here with the word for 'one' and *negonne* 'first'?) "TA example.: *annoonaeaeninnuog* 'messengers'", "formed on the theme 1 {g} of *annωn-* TA 'command, send (on a mission)' (v. *annωnaog*), with a passive meaning. TI examples.: *wussittumaenin* 'judge'", "*wussookhamwenin* 'writer'" (as can also be seen below "some TI formations make use of an extended derived initial ending in |-amwá-| (TI-1a), |-umwá-| (TI-1b)"and "|-awá-| (TI-2) {h} which may or may not be followed by |-w| ; |-á-| is sometimes dropped" and the presence of *-w-* following the |m| is dependent upon dialect. The suffix |-onk(an)| forms abstract and concrete nouns of instrument and so forth from AI and II stems and abstract nouns from TA and TI themes. Stems take |-u(w)|, |-ω|, |-oo| or |-ue| before adding this suffix. Examples: AI *anuhkasueonk* 'work', *nupwonk* 'death', II *wunnahteaonk* 'peace, friendship', TI *wussoohquahammooonk* 'writing', *wunnamptamooonk* 'faith'G&B1988.
28. To the top.

Examples in Cree:

- *ni-sākihāgan* 'my beloved' for *ni-sākihaw* 'I love him'.
- *ni-miswāgan* 'he whom I have wounded' for *ni-miswaw* 'I wound him'.

One forms **instrumental nouns** in Ojibway and Cree with the suffix *-gan* in connection with verbs in O. *-ge* and C. *-kew*.

[24]   Examples in Ojibway:

- *pakiteigan* 'hammer' for *pakiteige* 'he strikes'
- *tšigataigan* 'broom' for *tšigataige* 'sweep'.
- Examples is Cree:
- *tšikahigan* 'axe' for *tšikahikew* 'he chops wood'.
- *pākomosigan* 'emetic'[29] for *pākomosikew* 'he vomits'.[30]

Blackfoot has instrumental nouns, which are formed with the suffix *-atsĭs*:

- *ninikiatsĭs* 'musical instrument' for *ninikiu* 'he sings, he makes music'.
- *pokaiĭmatsĭs* 'fan' for *pokaiĭmau* 'he fans'.

An equivalent formation of Blackfoot occurs by the means of the suffix *-opi* with the simultaneous prefix of *it-*:

- *itaisĭnakiopi* 'pen' for *ai-sĭnakiu* 'he writes' (*ai* is prefix).
- *itaipĭksopi* 'hammer' for *ai-pĭksiu* 'he hammers' (*ai-* as in the previous example).

Ojibway forms deverbal locative nouns with the help of the suffix *-kan*. Such words are formed from verbs that end in *-ke*. Examples:

- *žominābokan* 'place where people make wine (vineyard)' for *žomināboke* 'he makes wine'.
- *biwābikokan* 'place where people produce iron (iron-mine)' for *biwābikoke* 'he produces iron'.

---

29. Vomit inducing medicine.
30. Beyond what has been said above for Natick under abstracts for the suffix |-onk(an)|, nouns of instrument and so forth are formed from TI verb stems by the means of the suffixes |-ēk(an)| (Examples: *paskehheg* 'gun', *kuhkinneek* 'boundary', *kwhkehhekanit* 'bounds (locative)') and |-onk(an)| (Examples: *uppaskohhonk* 'his/her gun', *wussuhquohhonk* 'writing', *kuhkinnonk* 'boundary').

I could name still more suffixes in the Algonquian-languages but the preceding is already sufficient to give an idea of the formation of the noun in this language family.

Adjectives

§ 20. The proper adjectives, which are not numerous in Ojibway are invariable and precede the nouns to which they provide an attribute. This applies completely the same to Cree and Blackfoot as to Ojibway. One often considers the prominent invariable attributive adjectives as inseparable prefixes, which at least for Blackfoot is quite defensible, since in this language some initial consonants of nouns are lost after such an invariable attributive element. Cree and Ojibway also agree with each other in the respect that the gradation here does not belong to the realm of morphology but rather to that of syntax, which for that matter can also be said for the other Algonquian languages.

Micmac and Natick vary quite sharply from Ojibway, Cree, and Blackfoot. Micmac has only well preserved one invariable adjective, which precedes the noun. The rest of the adjectives follow the noun and sometimes show agreement in the singular and regularly in the plural in gender and number. Invariable adjectives are also not completely foreign to Natick either, but agreement with the noun is the norm.

[25]

Examples of invariable adjectives:

- O. *minō*, C. *milo* 'good', O. *minō inini* 'a good man', *minō ikwēwag* 'good women', C. *milo ililiwak* 'good men'.
- O. C. *matši* 'bad', O. *matši abinōdziiad* 'bad children'. O.C. *matši manito* 'bad spirit'.
- O.C. *kitši* 'large', C. *kitši waskahigan* 'a large house'. M. *k(t)ši ulakan* 'a large dish'.
- O. *mitši*, C. *misi*, N. *mishe* 'large', N. *mishe wetu* 'large house'.
- B. *ŏkhsi* 'good', *ŏkhsi anikŏppi* 'a good young man' (:*manikŏppi* 'young man').
- Examples of completely or partially agreeing adjectives in Micmac:
- *meškilk* a. sing. *meškilkik* a. plur., *meškik* i. sing., *meškigal* i. plur. 'large'.
- *melkigenat* a. sing., *melkigenakik* a. plur., *melkigenak* i. sing., *melkigenal* i. plur. 'strong'.

- *afšeš* a. and i. sing., *afšešk* a. plur., *afšešgel* i. plur. 'small', *albadu afšeš* 'a small youth',
- *albaduk afšešk* 'small youths', *eptakan afšeš* 'a small plate', *eptakan'l afšešgel* 'little plates'.

Examples of agreeing adjectives in Natick:

- *wompesu* a. sing., *wompesuog* a. plur., *wompi* i. sing., *wompiyeuash* i. plur., 'white'.
- *mωesu* a. sing., *mωesuog* a. plur., *mωi* i. sing., *mωiyeuash* i. plur., 'black'.
- *menuhkesu* a. sing., *menuhkesuog* a. plur., *menuhki* i. sing., *menuhkiyeuash* i. plur., 'strong'
- *nωchumwesu* a. sing., *nωchumwesuog* a. plur., *nωchumwi* i. sing., *nωchumwiyeuash* i. plur., 'weak'.
- In Micmac, the adjective is subject to still other changes. If it has a negative adverb it undergoes a change of the suffix just as the substantives, as can be seen in the following example:
- *kelulk* sing., *kelulkel* i. plur., 'good, pretty', *mu kelultenu* sing., *mu kelultenugul* i. plur. 'not good, not pretty'.

[26] The adjectives in this language can also be provided with a preterite suffix. For example from the *kelulk* just mentioned one forms the preterites *kelulkšebenak* (a. sing.) and *kelulkšebenek* (i. sing.). The animate preterite plurals of *kigigu* 'old', *elueuit* 'bad' and *maleg* 'lazy' are respectively *kigiguuik*, *elueuišenik*, and *malekšebenik*.

Verbs with predicative adjectval meaning whose third person gerunds can be suffixed to the noun as an attribute -or perhaps I should speak rather, of apposition- play a much greater role in these languages than the actual adjectives. The form of the verb with an adjectival meaning varies according to whether the noun is animate or inanimate. The Natick adjectives just mentioned border on the true adjectives and adjectival-verbs, since various forms can be used as predicative and attributive at the same time. So *wompesa* a. is 'is white' as well as 'white'. In Micmac on the other hand the separation between adjectives and verbs is more sharply marked. It is self evident that the adjectival verbs, just as other verbs, are conjugated according to tenses, manners and so forth.

Examples in Ojibway:

- *maškawizi* a., *maškawa* i., 'is strong'.
- *sōngizi* a. *sōngan* i. 'is strong'.

- *manādizi* a., *manādad* i. 'is bad'.
- *onižiši* a., *onižišin* i. 'is pretty'.
- Examples in Cree:
- *miyosiw* a., *miwāsin* i. 'is pretty'.
- *pakwātikusiw* a., *pakwātikwan* i. 'is horrible'.
- Example in Micmac:
- *nil kelugi* 'I am good (pretty)', cf. the true adjective *kelulk*.
- Examples in Natick:
- *nωwompes* 'I am white', *wompiyeuω* 'it is white', cf. *wompi* 'white'.
- *nωchumwiyeu* 'it is weak', cf. *nωchumwi* 'weak'.
- Examples in Blackfoot:
- *mansiu* a. *maniu* i. 'is new'.
- *spĭksiu* a. *spĭkiu* i. 'is thick'.
- *ksĭksĭnŭm* a. *ksĭksĭnatsiu* i. 'is white'.

Numerals

§ 21. The treatment of the individual numerals belongs to the realm of lexicology rather than to that of morphology and only a general discussion serves here. If we compare the numerals in the various Algonquian languages it becomes immediately apparent to us that we have before us partially divergent ten-count systems, which are based on an original five-count system. However the similarity of the words for 'seven' and 'eight' in Natick and the word for 'ten' in Micmac to the equivalent numerals in Ojibway proves that the ten-count system had already developed in Proto-Algonquian and that the forms of the numerals 6-10 in Ojibway fairly reliably reflect the state in the earlier period of unity. Further more Ojibway and Cree have all sorts of particular points of agreement, which point to a quite close mutual relationship. Concerning the formation of the names for the multiples of 10, Micmac has two kinds of formation, one of which corresponds with Ojibway and Cree, and the other with Natick. More over, there also exist particular similarities between Micmac and Natick. The sharpest deviation is Blackfoot. I give only a comparative synopsis of the numerals 1-10 referring to the special grammars for the remainder. [27]

	O.	C.	M.	N.	B.
1	bežig, ningo	peyak, niko-	neukt, neuktešk neuktežit	nequt	nitŭkskŭm, sea
2	niž, nižo	niso, nišo, nižo	tabu	neese	natok(ŭm)
3	niswi, niso	nisto	tšišt, sist, nesidžik(-siskel)	nish	niok(skŭm)
4	nīwin, nīo	new(o)	neu	yau	nĭsso
5	nānan, nāno	niyānan, niyālal	nān	napanna tahshe	nĭsĭtto
6	ningotwāswi, ningotwāso	nikotwās(ik)	ažugom, asukom	nequtta tahshe	nau
7	nižwāswi	niswās, tepakup	i(l)uigeneuk	nesausuk tahshe	ikĭtsika
8	(n)išwāswi, (n)išwāswo	(a)yenānew	u(ge)mul(t) šin(-m)	shwosuk tahshe	nanĭsso
9	žāngaswi, žāngaso	šakitat, peyakostew, kekā(l)-mitāl(al)	peškunadek, peskunadek	paskoogun tahshe	pikso
10	midāswi, midāso, -(mi)dana	mitāl(al), -(mi)la-naw (-no)	mteln, -mteln, -inškak, -inskaak	piuk, -inchag	kepo, -ĭppo

The Micmac-forms *nesidžik* and *nesiskel* 'three' stand -next to each other- for animate and inanimate respectively and in Natick the element *tahshe* has the plural forms *tohsuog* (a.) and *tohsuash* (i.). In Blackfoot, the numerals have different endings, according to whether the attributives precede animate or inanimate words, e.g., *nitŭkskŭma ponokŏmita* 'one horse' (a.), *nitŭkskau oau* 'one egg' (i.), *natokŭmi ponokŏmitaks* 'two horses' (a.), *natokai oauĕsts* 'two eggs' (i.).

If numerals are used predicatively in Algonquian they take the form of a verb. Just as we observe in other intransitive verbs, the endings are then different for the two genders e.g., O. *nin-bežig* 'I am one (alone)', *bežigo* 'he (a.) is one (alone)': *bežigwan* 'it (i.) is one (alone)'; *nin-nižiman* 'we are two', *nižiwag* 'they (a.) are two': *nižinon* 'they (i.) are two'; C. *ni-peyakun* 'I am one (alone)', *peyakuw* 'he (a.) is one (alone)': *peyakwan* 'it (i.) is one (alone)'; *nižiwok* 'they (a.) are two': *nižinwa* 'they (i.) are two'. A similar situation is also prevalent in Natick and Blackfoot, however I am uncertain regarding Micmac. Nevertheless it is quite probable that animate and inanimate are distinguished in numeric verbs of this language as well.

Often times in Ojibway, the numerals are provided with classifying supplements and help words, which vary according to the nature of the form for the numbered objects. Similar types of indicative affixes of the numerals abound in other Algonquian languages as well, but I do not have sufficient information concerning their distribution outside of Ojibway.

§ 22. Reduplicated forms of the cardinal numbers are employed as **distributives** in Ojibway and Cree. In Cree the reduplicated vowel of the distributives is that variety of the stem vowels, which we indicate with the name **mutated vowel** (see §§ 30-32). In Ojibway, however we keep finding the reduplicated-syllables of these forms vocalized with *e*. Thus Cree has *pāpeyak* 'one by one', *nānižo* 'two by two', *nānisto* 'three by three', Ojibway in contrast has *bēbežig*, *nēniž* and *nēniswi*, In the same way O. *nibiwa* 'many' and *pangi* 'few' have the distributive reduplicated-forms *nēnibiwa* and *pēpangi*.

The iterative adverbs of Ojibway are derived from the usually shortened cardinal numbers with the suffix -*ing* (eg. *nižing* 'twice', *nising* 'thrice', *nīwing* 'four times', *nāning* 'five times'), but *ābiding* is used for 'once'. If the iteratives are reduplicated they acquire an additional distributive connotation (*nēnižing* 'twice each time', *nēnising* 'three times each time'). The distributive form of *ābiding* is *aiābiding* with vowel mutation.[31]

---

31. Acording to Uhlenbeck's BG from 1938 pg 129 the iteratives in Blackfoot are nearly all identical with the (i.) cardinals. From pg 119: *tókskai* 'once', *nátokai* 'twice', *niuókskai* 'thrice', *nisóyi* (*nisoái*) 'four times', *nisitóyi* 'five times', *náuyi* 'six times', *ixkitsikaii* 'seven times', *nánisoyi* 'eight times', *pixksóyi* 'nine times', *kepóyi* 'ten times'.

The only non-compounded ordinal number in Ojibway is *nitam* 'the first' or 'first', which corresponds to *nistam* in Cree. In Ojibway, the rest of the ordinals are formed, by providing the iterative with the prefix *ēko-*. In Cree, one can use cardinals with a preceding *iyaskutš* as ordinal numbers. The ordinals in Micmac are characterized by the suffix *-euei* (*-ewe*) added to the cardinals (e.g., *tabueuei* or *tabuewe* 'second, the second'), however for 'the first' or 'first' one finds various forms which are not derived from the numeral 'one'. Concerning the ordinals of Natick and Blackfoot, I am not sufficiently certain.[32]

---

32. According to Uhlenbeck's BG from 1938 pg 127, except for 'first', ordinal numbers in Blackfoot are formed by adding the prefix *omoχt(s)-* in conjunction with the suffix *-pi*(a.) or *-χpi*(i.). The (i.) forms are quite common while the (a.) forms seem rare. "Quite different in formation from these relative verbal forms are *matómoχt, matómoχtsi* (as prefix *matom~, ~atom~*) 'first'; *nátsáuχt, nátsáuχtsi* (as prefix *nats~*) 'last'; *sakóóχt, sakóóχtsi* (as prefix *sako~, sakoi~*) 'last'."
  All of these may be used as adverbs.
  Here are Uhlenbeck's (i.) ordinals from 1938 for first-tenth.
  First: *matómoχtsi*
  Second: *ómoχtsistòkaχpi*
  Third: *ómoχtsokskaχpi*
  Fourth: *ómoχtsìsoχpi*
  Fifth: *ómoχtsisìoχpi*
  Sixth: *ómoχtauoχpi*
  Seventh: *ómoχtauχtkitsìkoχpi*
  Eighth: *ómoχtànisoχpi*
  Ninth: *ómoχtsipìχksoχpi*
  Tenth: *ómoχtsippoχpi*

2. PRONOUNS

General remarks

§ 23. The chapter on pronouns provides relatively little difficulty and can be treated in just a few pages. A particular group is formed by the personal pronouns, to which the distinction for animate and inanimate is not known and which are pluralized by means of peculiar suffixes. For the first person plural we find the distinction of an exclusive and an inclusive form, for which there is a noticeable connection of the first person singular to the exclusive, and the second person singular to the inclusive. The pronominal prefixes of the verb and the possessive prefixes of the noun, which we have already dealt with, are either identical to the personal pronouns or closely related to them. The prefixed pronouns, either in the conjugation or in the possessive inflections, are the same for the singular and the plural and only from the accompanying suffixes can one tell if they are meant to be plural.

For the rest of the pronouns the distinction of animate and inanimate again treads to the foreground. Namely one uses varying pronouns, according to whether one is speaking of an animate being or an inanimate object.

The pronouns, with the exception of the personals, have a subordinate form or obviative where the dialect requires it just like the nouns. In addition it is noticeable that the pronominal obviative of Cree often has the form of a subobviative (cf. §§ 10-11). If we have true obviatives before us, then the forms in Ojibway and Cree also usually vary by infixing the characterizing element of the nouns. The same applies for some plural forms, which have the plural inflection in the middle of the word. We find infixed pluralization on an even greater scale for the pronouns of Blackfoot.

Personals (possesives) [30]

§ 24. The individual personal pronouns in the languages being treated here are:

First person.

- sing. ' I ': O. *nin*, C. *ni(l)a*, M. *nin, nil*, N. *neen*, B. *něstoa*.
- plur.; excl. 'we': O. *ninawind*, C. *ni(l)anān, ni(l)ān*, M. *ninen*, N. *neenawun*, B. *něstŭnan*.
- plur. incl. 'we': O. *kinawind*, C. *kilanānow, ki(l)ānow*, M. *kinu*, N. *kenawun*, B. *kěstŭnan*.

Second person.

- sing. 'you': O. *kin*, C. *ki(l)a*, M. *kil*, N. *ken*, B. *k(s)ěstoa*. plur. 'you', O. *kinawa*, C. *ki(l)awaw*, M. *kilau*, N. *kenaau*, B. *kěstoau*.

Third person.

- sing. 'he': O. *win*, C. *wi(l)a*, M. *negeum*, N. *noh, nagum*, B. *ostoi*.
- plur. 'they': O. *winawa*, C. *wi(l)awaw*, M. *negmau*, N. *nahoh, nagoh*, B. *ostoauai*.

As one sees, the personal pronouns of Blackfoot have deviated far from the Proto-Algonquian type. Concerning M. *negeum*, N. *noh, nagam*, plur. M. *negmau*, N. *nahoh, nagoh*, this is actually a demonstrative that is employed as a personal pronoun.

The prefixed personal (possessive) pronouns are as follows:

First person.

- sing. and plur.: excl.: O. *nin(d)-, nidž-, ni-,n-*, C. *ni(t)-, n-*, M. *n-*, N. *n+* vowel, *n-*, B. *nit-, nĭt(s)-, no-, ni-, n-*.
- plur. incl.: O. *ki(d)-, kidž-, k-*, C. *ki(t)-, ki-*, M. *k-*, N. *k+* vowel, *k-*, B. *kit-, kĭt(s)-, ko-, ki-, k-*.

Second person.

- sing. and plur. O. *ki(d)-, kidž-,* k-, C. *ki(t)-, k-*, M. *k-*, N. *k+* vowel, *k-*, B. *kit-, kĭt(s)-, ko-, ki-, k-*.

Third person.

- sing. and plur.: O. *o(d)-, widž-, w-*, C. *o(t)-, w-*, M. *u-*, N. *w+*vowel, *w-*, B *ot-, ots-, o-*.

[31] In the conjugation Ojibway uses *nin(d)-, ki(d)-,* and *o(d)-* exclusively, which however also serve as possessive prefixes. Concerning

Blackfoot, *nit-*, *kit-*, and *ot-* are the prevowel forms of *ni-*, *ki-*, and *o-* for the verbs. The prevowel prefixes of the noun are *nĭt(s)-*, *kĭt(s)-*, *ot(s)* and *n-*, *k-*, *o-*. In certain verbal forms, which are characterized by initial-vowel conjugation prefixes Blackfoot does not use *nit-* and *kit-* but rather *n-* and *k-*. Concerning the third person prefix it should be noted that in the conjugation of the Algonquian-languages it is almost exclusively limited to the portion of the transitive forms of this person with incorporated subjects and objects. I shall not expand further upon the extent to which prefixes are used in the dialects treated here, but I cannot neglect to mention that there are considerable differences present. For instance the third-person-prefix plays a much less important role in Cree than Ojibway.

Besides *o(t)-* Blackfoot has still another third-person-prefix, *m-*, the use of which parallels that of *n-* and *k-*. We find this in certain forms of the intransitive as well as in the transitive conjugations.

Although there are 'one'-forms present in the verb of the Algonquian dialects there is no prefix that corresponds to our 'one'.

The pluralization of the prefixes by the means of simultaneously appearing suffixes need not be discussed here. Concerning the possessive prefixes cf. §§ 12-14, concerning the personal prefixes of the verb see § 49.

Other pronouns

§ 25. In the first place I will provide an overview of the **demonstratives**, which are quite divergent in the various Algonquian languages.

This a.
- O. *aw, waaw, māba(m)*; obv. *māmin*; plur. *ogōw, māmig*.
- C. *awā*; obv. *oho*; plur. *oki, oko*.
- N. *yeuoh*; plur. *yeug*.
- B. *amom, amoiă; amoksĭm, amoksi*.

This i.
- O. *ow, māndan*; plur. *onōw, iniw*.
- C. *oma*; obv. sing. *omeliw*; plur. *ohi, oho*; obv. plur. *omeliwa*.
- N. *yeu*; plur. *yeush*.
- B. *amom, amoiă*; plur. *amostsim, amostsi*.

That a.

- O. *aw*; obv. *iniw, aniw*; plur. *igiw, agiw*.
- C. *anā* (*nāhā*); obv. *anihi*; plur. *aniki* (*nekī*)
- N. *noh, nagum*; plur. *nahoh, nagoh, nag, neg*.
- B. *omŭm*; *omĭksĭm, omĭksĭk*.

That i.

- O. *iw*; plur. *iniw*.
- C. *ani, anima* (*nema*); obv. *aniheliw, animeliw*; plur. *anihi* (*nehi*); obv. plur. *aniheliwa, animeliwa*.
- N. *ne*; plur. *nish*.
- B. *omim*; plur. *omistsĭm*.

Concerning Micmac I cannot sufficiently determine the boundary between animate and inanimate. Therefore I give only the forms without an attempt in turn to sort them:

- *ut, ula; negeum, na; āt, alā;* plur. *weget, negala, negula, egula, wakela, wagela, wegula, wogula, wola.*[33]

Cree has still another demonstrative *e(w)oko,* which is animate as well as inanimate and of which obviative and plural forms are also in use. I am unable however to deduce the meaning with absolute certainty from the material that I am familiar with.

In general there are great differences observable between the forms in the languages being treated here. O. *aw* a. and *ow* i. appear to be related to each other and to stand in further relation with C. *awā* a. and N. *yeuoh* a., *yeu* i. Also O. *iw* will, in one way or another have something to do with this group. The *g* of the plural in O. *ogōw, igiw, agiw* is apparently the plural inflection of the animate gender, while we can see the plural inflection of the inanimate gender in the *n* of the plural O. *onōw, iniw.* O. *ogōw* corresponds with C. *oko,* but beyond this there is very little agreement between

---

33. Proulx Micmac
    Invariable demonstratives
    u:t 'this'
    a:t 'that'
    Ocasionaly inflected
    ula 'this'
    ala 'that'

the plural forms of the demonstratives in both of these languages. It is however apparent that the *k* in C. *oki, aniki* and *neki* is also the plural inflection of the animate gender. The plural of the inanimate gender C. *oho, ohi, anihi* and *nehi* exhibit an *h-* not *n-* as the plural inflection, but the comparison of *oho* with O. *onōw* shows the loss of *n* in Cree, so that the *h* has developed as a vowel separator. We also find an *h* in the obviative. It is odd that O. *māmin* and *māmig*, which appear to be connected etymologically with *māba(m)* and the inanimate *māndan*, have the *n* of the obviative and the *g* of the plural as terminations just like the nouns and some pronouns to be discussed later (cf. forms like N. *yeug, nahoh, yeush* and *nish*), by [33] which obviatives like *iniw* and *aniw* and plurals like *ogōw, igiw, agiw, onōw* and *iniw* (also like B. *amoksĭm, amoksi, amostsĭm, amostsi, omiksĭm, omiksĭk* and *omistsĭm*) distinguish themselves. I also find it unexplainable why the obviatives of some of the demonstrative pronouns in Cree terminate in *-liw(a)*, which is the inflection of the subobviative or the double subordinated form of the nouns. From the preceding, it is apparent in each case that the demonstratives of Ojibway and Cree, despite great deviation, still have points of agreement. On the other hand perhaps C. *oma* can be compared with B. *amom, omŭm* and *omim*. We should also consider the relationship of C. *anā, ani, anima* and *nema* with N. *noh, nagum* and *ne*, and M. *negeum* and *na*. In no case does the *n* of the mentioned Cree forms have anything to do with the O. forms of *aniw*, which -as we have already seen- is the obviative inflection. Concerning N. *noh* and *nagum*, and M. *negeum* cf. § 24 (third person).

§ 26. I now continue to the **interrogatives**.

'Who?' a.

- O. *awēnen*; obv. *awēnenan*; plur. *awēnenag*.
- C. *awena, awewa*; obv. *aweliwa (aweyiwa), awenihi*; plur. *aweniki*.
- M. *wen*; plur. *wenik*.
- N. *howan*; plur. *howanig*.
- B. *tŭkka*.

'What?' i.

- O. *wegonen, anin*.
- C. *kekwan, kekwai*; obv. *kekwa(ni)liw*; plur. *kekwana, kekwaya*.

- M. *kokuei*, pl. *kokuel*.
- N. *chagwas, shaugwas, teagua, toh*.
- B. *tsa, åksa*.

'Which?' a.

- C. *tān(a)*, obv. *tān(a) anihi*, plur. *tān(a) aniki*.
- M. *tān*, plur. *tānik*.
- B. *taa* (of plur.), *tŭma, taia* (of two); plur. *tsiktsĭma, tsiktsea*.

'Which?' i.

- C. *tānima* (from *tan-anima*), *tāniwe*; obv. *tānimāyiw, tāniweyiw*; plur. *tāniwehe*.
- M. *tān*; plur. *tānel*.
- N. *tanyeu, uttiyeu*; plur. *uttiyeush*.
- B. *taa* (of plural), *tsĭma, tsia* (of two) plur. *tsĭstsĭma, tsĭstsea*.[34]

[34] In Cree we also find still another *keko* 'what kind?'. a. i. plur. *kekwayak*.

One can see that some similarity exists. The most divergent is Blackfoot, although even here the so wide spread stem *tān(a)* is represented by *taa*. Striking is the similarity of O. *awēnen* with Cree, Micmac and Natick, and the mutual relationship between C. *kekwan, kekwai*, and *keko* and M. *kikuei* can also not be doubted. In contrast with almost all demonstratives, the interrogative O. *awēnen* forms the obviative and the plural in the same manner as nouns, but in B. *tsiksĭma, tsiksea* and *tsĭstsĭma, tsĭstsea* the plural inflections -*ks*- and -*sts*- are not terminations. This is in agreement with that which we have said concerning the plural formation of demonstratives in Blackfoot. In Natick *howan* and *uttiyeu* are pluralized with the help of nominal suffixes, just as the demonstratives and M. *wenik, tānik, kokuel* and *tānel* also exhibit this same type. Concerning the obviatives of Cree one can compare the previous paragraph.

I mention further, as a peculiarity, that M. *wen* and *tān* possess temporal forms in both numbers.

---

34. Proulx Micmac
    Interogatives
    koxowey 'what'
    ta:n 'when'
    teken 'which'

§ 27. In Ojibway relative clauses are rendered by personal gerunds so there is no need for **relatives**. There are also no relative pronouns present in Cree, the deficiency of which can be filled by syntactic means. One of these means is the use of the relative particle *ka*.

In Micmac one employs the interrogatives *wen* and *tān*, in Natick the demonstratives *noh* and *ne* are also used as relatives.

In Blackfoot however we find separate relatives:

- 'That' a.: *annŏk*; plur. *anniksĭsk*.
- 'That' i.; *annik*; plur. *annistsĭsk*.

Perhaps *annŏk* and *annik*, which are reminiscent of C. *anā* and *ani*, were originally demonstrative. Concerning the plural forms *anniksĭsk* and *annistsĭsk* we also find that the plural inflections *-ks-* and *-sts-* are not terminations but infixes.

Our relative 'what, which, that which', is expressed in Blackfoot by affixing *-pi* to the verbal form.

§ 28. There is no reason to sum up all of the remaining pronouns because one can refer to the dictionaries of the various languages. The indefinites of the Algonquian languages mutually deviate strongly, but Ojibway and Cree nevertheless have some in common.

- '**Someone.**'[35] a.: O. *awiia*, C. *awiyak*.
- '**No-one.**' a.: O. *ka(win) awiia*, C. *nama awiyak*.
- '**All.**' a. i.: O. *kakina*, C. *kakiyaw*.

[35]

But O. *awēgwen* 'who also'. a. and *wēgotogwen* 'what also'. i. appear to have no related forms in Cree. On the other hand Cree possesses indefinites, which we do not find in Ojibway.

I mention further that B. *stsĭki* 'other'. a. i. pluralizes in termination just as the noun: *stsĭksiks* a. and *sisĭkists* i. Fairly surprising are the Blackfoot forms for 'many': *akaiem*. a., *akauo*. i.

---

35. Or perhaps also [anyone].

3. VERBS

General remarks

§ 29. Besides the contrast between transitive and intransitive, the distinction of animate and inanimate also comes to the foreground in the conjugation. As a rule, the intransitive verbs vary according to whether their subject is animate or inanimate, and they also correspond in number to that subject, but the transitive verbs agree in gender with their object and in number with both their subject and object. Impersonal verbs are treated as intransitives with an inanimate subject. Where subordinative forms are present, these are also reflected in the verbal forms. For the transitive verb, we find active and passive forms. The verbs of the Algonquian languages also have reflexives and reciprocals, next to all kinds of other secondary verbs.

In all of the dialects of this language group, the personal prefixes are related to each other and to the possessive prefixes as well as the independent pronouns. In contrast, the terminations of the verbs are quite uneven in the various modes and the various languages.

Concerning numbers, the presence of a dual can be established in Micmac.

Incorporation is present on a large scale. Apart from the incorporation of subject and object, incorporation of the indirect object is not completely foreign to some languages. We even find the nominal object incorporated in the verb here and there.

Algonquian possesses various modes, which by their character are reminiscent of those in our own language family. Less familiar in contrast is the dubiative conjugation, which fulfills such a large role in Ojibway, Cree and Blackfoot. Beyond this, many Algonquian languages express the contrast of affirmative and negative in the verbal form and Natick as well as Blackfoot has an interogative conjugation besides.

[36]

The distinction of time and aspect are also made known in the verb. In Algonquian, prefixes play the chief role in the temporal inflexion.

Peculiar to Algonquian is the formation of personal gerunds (participles) by vowel alteration in the initial syllable of the conjunctive forms, regardless of whether the syllable is root-based or a prefix. In Blackfoot, where these mutations no longer appear to fulfill a grammatical role, a -k suffix is added to the verbal forms in relative clauses.

Mutation

§ 30. The **mutation**, which I have just mentioned is of great importance, especially in Ojibway and Cree, not only for the formation of personal gerunds, but also in certain other cases that I will sum up shortly, but of which it can be said in general that they convert to a distributive, iterative and intensive fundamental idea that is expressed in many languages by complete or partial reduplication. There are also secondary verbs with distributive and iterative meanings in Algonquian dialects, which exhibit reduplication of the initial consonant and mutation in the reduplicating syllable. The distributive numerals of Cree and to a certain extent those of Ojibway, are of this same type. Could the original situation, not be preserved in such cases and could the mutation not be explained everywhere, by the vowel differentiation with reduplication of the initial consonant? We must then assume that the forms starting with a vowel have undergone several contractions of the reduplicating vowel with the initial vowel and the forms with a consonant at the beginning had lost her inter-vocalic after the reduplicating syllable, either by phonetic change or by analogical influence from the initial-vowel forms. This process could have already taken place in Proto-Algonquian, for where we cannot show the mutation we have reason to suspect this was once there. One finds traces in Deleware for example, but in Micmac and Natick I have not yet been able to discover them. Further investigation shall probably show that traces are present here as well. Concerning Blackfoot, one can compare *nanïsso* 'eight': with *nïsso* 'four', but the peculiar vowel changes in certain cases of the conjugation of this language (eg. -o-: i-) do not belong to the sphere of Algonquian mutation and also fulfill entirely different grammatical functions.

§ 31. I give here a survey of the mutation in Ojibway and Cree, in the hopes that, with the help of other dialects, one will be able to reconstruct those of Proto-Algonquian.

- O. C. *ā*, mutated O. *aiā*, C. *eyā*, *iyā*, e.g., O. *ākosi*, C. *ākusiw* 'he is sick', mutated O. *aiākosid*, C. *eyākusit*, 'he being sick, he that is sick'.
- O. C. *a*, mutated O. *ē*. C. *e*, e.g., O. *abī*, C. *apiw*, 'he is', mutated O. *ēbid*, C. *epit* 'he that is'.
- O. *ē*, C. *e* mutated O. *aiē*, C. *iye*, e.g., O. *dēbwe* 'he speaks the truth', C. *tepwew* 'he shouts, calls', mutated O. *daiēbwed* 'he that speaks the truth', C. *tiyepwet* 'he that shouts, calls'.
- O. C. *ī*, mutated O. *ā*, C. *iye*, e.g., O. *nīmi*, C. *nīmiw* 'he dances' mutated O. *nāmid*, C. *niyemit* 'he that dances'.
- O. C. *i*, mutated O. *ē*, C. *e*, e.g., O. *nibō*, C. *nipuw* (*nipiw*) 'he dies, is dead', mutated O. *nēbod*, C. *neput* 'he that is dead'.
- O. C. *ō*, mutated O. *wā* C. *iyo*, e.g., O. *bōsi*, C. *pōsiw* 'he embarks', mutated O. *bwāsid*, C. *piyosit* 'he that embarks'.
- O. C. *o*, mutated O. *wē*, C. *we*, e.g., O. *ogimāwi*, *okimāwiw* 'he is chief' mutated O. *wēgimāwid*, C. *wekimāwit* 'he that is chief'.

In Ojibway there are some verbs with initial *d* that in place of the usual mutation, prefix the syllable *en*, but many other verbs that begin with *d* have the usual mutation.

If a verb in Ojibway or Cree is provided with a prefix or, if an adverb preceedes it, then, in the case of mutation, the vowel of the prefix or that of the adverb is mutated. With respect to the mutation, the prefixed personal elements of the verb are not considered prefixes but rather as individual words. To clear this up I give a few examples:

- O. *nin-wābama* 'I see him', *nin-waiābamag* 'I that sees him'; *nin-gī-wābama* 'I have seen him', *nin-gā-wābamag* 'I that have seen him'; *nin-ga-wābama* 'I shall see him', *nin-gē-wābamag* 'I that shall see him'.
- O. *nin-bī-ižā* 'I come here', *nin-bā-ižāiānin* ' when[36] I come here';[37] *bī-ižā* 'he comes here', *bā-ižādžig* 'they that come here'.
- O. *minō-bimādizi* 'he lives well', *mēno-bimādizid* 'he that lives well'.

It shall not be necessary to give separate examples for Cree as well. I will however show, with a few cases, how great the agreement is between Cree and Ojibway:

---

36. In the sense of 'whenever'.
37. This is the iterative conjunct formed by vowel mutation and *-in* suffix, see § 41.

O. *aiā*, C. *ayaw* 'he is', O. *eiād*, C. *eyāt* 'he that is'; O. *mino-aiā*, C. *miyo-ayaw* 'he is well', O. *meno-aiād*, C. *meyo-ayāt* 'that is well',[38] O. *kitši mino aiā*, C. *kitši miyow ayaw* 'he is quite well', O. *ketši-mino-aiād*, C. *ketši-miyo-ayāt* 'that is quite well';[39] O. *wi-kitši-mino-aiā*, C. *wi-kitši-miyo-ayaw* 'he wants to be quite well', O. *wa-kitši-mino-aiād*, C. *wa-kitši-miyo-ayāt* 'that desires to be quite well'[40] (the prefix *wi-* in Cree has mutation vowel *a*. which is irregular for this dialect).

§ 32. Ojibway uses the mutation in the following cases:
- 1° in all personal gerunds;
- 2° in the iterative conjunct;
- 3° if one wishes to give the impression that an event has just taken place;
- 4° after interrogative pronouns and adverbs;
- 5° to express the conjunction 'as' or 'like';
- 6° after some particles, which I shall not further specify here;
- 7° in some tenses for the conjunctive of the dubiative conjugation;
- 8° often times in the reduplicating syllables of secondary verbs with distributive, iterative or intensive meaning.

Most of these rules also apply for Cree, where moreover the reduplicating syllable of the distributive numerals, which is always vocalized with *e* in Ojibway, exhibits the regular mutation.

Concerning the first seven of the above cases, the mutated forms link up everywhere with the conjunctive. There are no independent forms or gerunds derived from the indicative.

Division of the verbs

§ 33. In Algonquian the verbs can be divided into the following main groups;

I   Intransitive verbs with animate subject.[41]
II Intransitive verbs with inanimate subject.[42]

---

38. (he)
39. (he)
40. (he)
41. (AI)
42. (II)

III Transitive verbs with animate object.[43]
IV Transitive verbs with inanimate object.[44]

The adjectival-verbs, which have already been discussed in § 20, belong to the first class in their animate form and to the second class in their inanimate form. From the nature of things the verbs of the second class, which also include the impersonal verbs, are only customary in the third person, for which reason they have been named uni-personals.

[39]

I begin with some examples of the four classes in **Ojibway**:

Class I.

- *nin-mādža* 'I depart', *mādža* 'he departs'.
- *nin-žāwendžige* 'I am compassionate', *žāwendžige* 'he is compassionate'.
- *nin-bōs* 'I embark', *bōsi* 'he embarks'.
- *nin-gīgit* 'I speak', *gīgito* 'he speaks'.
- *nind-inendam* 'I think', *inendam* 'he thinks'.
- *nin-dagwišin* 'I arrive', *dagwišin* 'he arrives'.

Class II.

- *ižinikāde* 'it is called', *ižinikādewan* 'they (i.) are called'.
- *kisinā(magad)* 'it is cold weather'.
- *sōgipo(magad)* 'it snows'.
- *sanagad* 'it is difficult, costly'.
- *anakwad* 'it is cloudy'.
- *onižišin* 'it is beautiful, good', *onižišinon* 'they (i.) are good, beautiful'.
- *sōngan* 'it is strong', *sōnganon* 'they (i.) are strong'.
- *nōdin* 'it is windy'.

Class III.

- *nin-wābama* 'I see him', *o-wābamān* 'he sees him'.
- *nin-sāgia* 'I love him', *o-sāgiān* 'he loves him'.
- *nind-ižānan* 'I visit him', *od-ižānan* 'he visits him'.
- *nind-atāwenan* 'I sell him', *od-atāwenan* 'he sells him'.
- Class IV.

---

43. (TA)
44. (TI)

- *nin-wābandān* 'I see it', *o-wābandān* 'he sees it'.
- *nin-minikwēn* 'I drink it', *o-minikwēn* 'he drinks it'.
- *nin-mīdžin* 'I eat it', *o-mīdžin* 'he eats it'.
- *nin-bidon* 'I bring it', *o-bidon* 'he brings it'.

Examples of the four classes in **Cree**:

Class I.

- *ni-nipān* 'I sleep', *nipaw* 'he sleeps'.
- *ni-pimotān* 'I walk', *pimotew* 'he walks'.
- *ni-miyosin* 'I am beautiful', *miyosiw* 'he is beautiful'.

Class II.

- *miwāsin* 'it is beautiful', *miwāsinwa* 'they (i.) are beautiful'.
- *kimiwan* 'it rains'.
- *mispun* 'it snows'.

Class III.

- *ni-wāpamaw* 'I see him', *wāpamew* 'he sees him'.
- *ni-sākihaw* 'I love him', *sākihew* 'he loves him'.

Class IV.

- *ni-wāpaten* 'I see it', *wāpatam* 'he sees it'.
- *ni-sākitān* 'I love it', *sākitaw* 'he love it'.

Examples of the four classes in Micmac:

Class I.

- *eim* 'I am', *eik* 'he is'.
- *amalkaye* 'I dance', *amalkat* 'he dances'.
- *nil kelugi* 'I am good, beautiful', *negeum kelugit* 'he is good, beautiful', *kelugidau* 'he shall be good, beautiful', *keludak* 'they (a.) shall be good, beautiful'.

Class II.

- *edek* 'it is'. *kelultedau* 'it shall be good, beautiful', *kelultedal* 'they (i.) shall be good, beautifull'.
- *pežak* 'it snows'.

Class III.

I have no clear paradigms at my disposal.

Class IV.

- *kebukuadem* 'I sew it'.

Examples of the four classes in **Natick:**

Class I.

- *nωwaantam* 'I am wise', *waantamnoh* 'he is wise'.
- *nωwompes* 'I am white', *wompesu* 'he is white'.

Class II.

- *wompiyeω* 'it is white'.
- *nωchumwiyeu* 'it is weak'.

Class III.

- *nωwadchan* 'I keep him', *ωwadchanuh* 'he keeps him'.

Class IV.

- *nωwadchanumun* 'I keep it'.

Examples of the four classes in **Blackfoot:**

Class I.

- *nit-ai-oka* 'I sleep', *ai-okau* 'he sleeps'.
- *nit-ŭkometŭkki* 'I love', *ŭkometŭkkiu* 'he loves'.
- *mansiu* 'he is new'.

Class II.

- *maniu* 'it is new'.
- *ai-sotau* 'it rains'.
- *åkhputau* 'it snows'.

Class III. [41]

- *nit-ŭkomĭmmau* 'I love him', *ŭkomĭmmiuaie* 'he loves him'.

Class IV.

- *nit-ŭkometsip* 'I love it', *ŭkometsĭmaie* 'he loves it'.

Verbal types

§ 34. The right forms that apply as **passives** in Algonquian are characterized by peculiar personal terminations. Examples:

- O. *nin-wābamigo* 'I am seen', cf. *nin-wābamig* 'he sees me'.
- O. *ki-wābamigo* 'you (sing.) are seen', cf. *ki-wābamig* 'he sees you (sing.)'.
- O. *wābama* 'he is seen', *o-wābamigon* 'he is seen' (by a certain person), cf. *o-wābamān* 'he sees him'.
- B. *nit-siksioko* 'I am bitten', cf. *nit-siksipok* 'he bites me'.
- B. *kit-siksipoko* 'you (sing.) are bitten', cf. *kit-siksipok* 'he bites you (sing.)'.
- B. *siksipau* 'he is bitten', cf. *ai-siksipiuaie* 'he bites him'.

I have placed the Blackfoot examples immediately under those of Ojibway to make it apparent how much the formation of the passive corresponds between these two languages, which in other regards are so far removed from each other. Related passive forms in -*ko* are also present in Cree, e.g., *ni-wāpamiko, ki-wāpamiko* but I am uncertain concerning their exact meaning. As one says, they are being used preteritely and are equivalent with forms in -*kotai,* which have an unquestinably preterite function. Forms such as C. *wāpamaw* 'he is seen', *mowaw* 'he is eaten', N. *wadchanau* 'he is kept' are however in complete agreement with O. *wābamaw,* and B. *siksipau* in form and function. Cree has still another passive formation as well e.g., *ni-mowikawin* 'I am eaten', *ki-mowikawin* 'you (sing.) are eaten', *ni-mowikawin* 'I was being eaten'. Still further passive forms of Natick are *nωwadchanit* 'I am kept', *kωwadchanit* 'you (sing.) are kept'. The passive of Micmac is completely divergent: *nemikugi* 'I am seen', *ankodaši* 'I am guarded.

§ 35. One also finds **reflexive** verbs in Algonquian. Those of Ojibway are formed by means of a suffix -*s(o)* or (-*i*)*dizo*, e.g., *nin-babāmitas* 'I obey myself': *ninbāmitawa* 'I obey him': *nin-nōndās* 'I hear myself': *nin-nōndawa* 'I hear him'; *nin-kikēnindiz* 'I know myself'; *nin-kikēnima* 'I know him'; *nin-wābandiz* 'I see myself': *nin-wābama* 'I see him'; *nin-minaidiz* 'I give myself water': *nin-minaa* 'I give him water'. One can see from the third person and the plural forms that there was once an *o* after the sibilant.

Other dialects also have a reflexive verb, e.g., C. *ni-sāki-hisun* 'I love myself', M. *nemiši* 'I see myself', B. *nit-ŭkomĭmmosi* 'I love myself'

The reflexives are to be distinguished from the **reciprocals**, which are found in the various Algonquian-languages. In Ojibway they are characterized by the suffix *-di-* which appears to be related to the reflexive *-(i)diz(o)*. e.g., *nin-nōndadimin* 'we hear each other', *nin-nisitotadimin* 'we understand each other'. At present I will not speak concerning the reciprocals in Cree and so forth.

Mood representations

§ 36. In the Algonquian languages we have to distinguish between general and particular mode representations. Under general mood representations I understand the affirmative, negative and interrogative; with the special mood representations I mean the actual modes. On the border between both stands the dubitative mode representation, which does not however appear to be represented by separate forms in Micmac and Natick.[45] Concerning the actual modes we find the indicative, conjuctive and imperative everywhere, while the optative, potential and conditional are not found in all of the languages dealt with here. I will discuss the personal gerunds of Ojibway and Cree in relation with the conjunctive.

§ 37. In Ojibway the **negative** conjugation is derived from the affirmative with the help of the suffix *-si(-)* immediately following the verbal stem. The particle *kawin* 'not' precedes the negative verb, except in the imperative, where one employs the prohibitive *kego* in place of *kawin*. If we compare Cree we see that the negative conjugation of Ojibway has developed out of a diminutive. In Cree where no negative conjugation is present we nevertheless still find the same *-si(-)* element, but here it only diminishes the meaning of a verb. e.g., C. *minikwe-si-n* 'I drink a little bit', *minikwe-si-iw* 'he drinks a little bit', *nipi-si-n* 'I sleep a little bit', *nipe-si-w* 'he sleeps a little

---

45. This is not entirely accurate. Micmac does appear to have as many as perhaps three dubiatives, one of which appears to be related to the interrogative conjugations of both Micmac and Natick. See §§ 38-39.

bit'. Therefore it is also quite explainable that the negative forms of Ojibway are preceded by *kawin* or *kego*. After all one says *kawin nind-inendansi* 'I think not', which had then originally meant 'not think I a bit' ('I do not think even a bit' = 'I do not think at all'). One can rightly bring O. C. -*si*(-) — in Cree also -*ši*(-) — in to relation with diminutive -*s* or -*š* suffix of the nouns.

I give some more examples of the negative forms in Ojibway:

- *kawin nind-ikkitosi* 'I say not': *nind-ikkit* 'I say'.
- *kawin kid-inendānsim* 'you (plur.) think not': *kid-inendām* 'you (plur.) think'.
- *kawin dagwišininsim* 'one does not arrive': *dagwišinim* 'one arrives'.
- *kawin nin-wābamasiwanaban* 'we (excl.) we saw him not': *nin-wābamanaban* 'we (excl.) saw him'.
- *kego ikkitosida* 'let us not say': *ikkitoda* 'let us say'.
- *kego o-ga-wābamasin* 'let him not see him': *o-ga-wābamān* 'let him see him'.

Only in the second person of the imperative does Ojibway have negative forms which do not contain the element -*si*(-), e.g., *kego ikkitoken* 'say not': *ikkito(ka)n* 'say', *kego ikkitokegon* 'say not': *ikkito(io)g, ikkitokeg* 'say', *kego wābamāken* 'see him not': *wābam(ākan)* 'see him', *kego wābamakegon* 'see him not': *wābamig* 'see him'.

The personal terminations of the negative verb are often not completely identical to those of the affirmative verb. There are also some differences between the affirmative and negative terminations in Micmac, where the negative forms are almost regularly characterized by the infixing or suffixing of a *u* and by far in most cases they are usually preceded by the particle *mu*. One need only compare the conjugation of *mu amalkau* 'I dance not ' with that of *amalkaye* 'I dance'.

		Affirmative	Negative
1	sing.	amalkaye	mu amalkau
2	sing.	amalkan	mu amalkaun
3	sing.	amalkat	mu amalkauk
1	du. e.	amalkayek	mu amalkayek

		Affirmative	Negative
1	du. i.	amalkayku	mu amalkayku
2	du.	amalkayok	mu amalkauok
3	du.	amalkagik	mu amalkauk
1	pl. e.	amalkaldiek	mu amalkaldiuek
1	pl. i.	amalkaldiku	mu amalkaldiku
2	pl.	amalkaldiok	mu amalkaldiuok
3	pl.	amlakaldigik	mu amalkaldiuk

The negative future of Micmac is similar to the negative present, [44] but as a negative particle, it is not preceded by *mu*, but by *man*, e.g., *man amalkau* 'I shall not dance'; *amalkadeš* 'I shall dance', *man ygau* 'I shall not strike': *ygadeš* 'I shall strike'.

In Natick one finds a related negative conjugation, which is characterized in general by the infixing or suffixing of ω. This becomes apparent from the comparison of the paradigm: *nωwaantamωh* 'I am not wise' with the corresponding affirmative forms.

		Affirmative	Negative
1	sing.	nωwaantam	nωwaantamωh
2	sing.	kωwaantam	kωwaantamωh
3	sing.	waantamnoh	waantamωh
1	pl. e.	nωwaantamumun	nωwaantamωmun
1	pl. i.		
2	pl.	kωwaantamumwω	kωwaantamωmwω
3	pl.	waantamwog	waantamωog

Also *nωwadchanumωun* 'I do not keep it': *nωwadchanumun* 'I keep it', *nωwadchanòh* 'I do not keep him': *nωwadchan* 'I keep him' etc. Sometimes there are considerable differences to be established between the negative and affirmative terminations, e.g., *nωwadchanumωunnonup* 'we[46] do not keep it': *nωwadchanumumun* 'we[47] keep it', *kωwadchanumωwop* 'you (pl.) do not keep it': *kωwadchanumumwω* 'you (pl.) keep it'.

The negative particle, which in certain cases precedes the negative verbal forms of Natick, is *mat*. This element also turns up again in the negative conjugation of Blackfoot, which nevertheless exhibits quite mutually divergent prefixing and suffixing formations in various modes and tenses.

Some examples of these will not be superfluous:

- *ni-mat-ŭkometŭkkipa* 'I do not love': *nit-ŭkometŭkki* 'I love'.
- *mat-ŭkometŭkkiuats* 'he does not love': *ŭkometŭkkiu* 'he loves'.
- *ni-mat-ŭkomĭmmauats* 'I do not love him': *nit-ŭkomĭmmau* 'I love him'.
- *ni-mat-ŭkomĭmmauaksau* 'I do not love them': *nit-ŭkomĭmmaiau* 'I love them'.
- *pin-ŭkometŭkkĭt* 'do not love': *ŭkometŭkkit* 'love'.
- *ŏk-stai-ŭkometŭkkiop* 'let us (incl.) not love': *ŏk-ŭn-ŭkometŭkkiop* 'let us (incl.) love'.
- *sau-ŭkometŭkkieniki* 'if I love not': *ŭkometŭkkieniki* 'if I love' (One also uses the same forms in the second person).
- *ni-kŭtta-ŭkometŭkkitopi* 'if I loved not': *nit-ŭkometŭkkitopi* 'if I loved'.

§ 38. Of the languages being treated here both Natick and Blackfoot have an **interrogative** conjugation.[48]

In Natick the interrogative is made from the affirmative by suffixing *-as* (*-us*), but one can see from the following paradigms that irregularities still present themselves there. For comparison I have set the conjugation of *nωwadchanumun* 'I keep it' next to that of *nωwadchanumunás* 'do I keep it?'

---

46. (excl.)
47. (excl.)
48. Micmac appearently has an interrogative conjugation with the same vowel + s suffix as in Natick below. In Micmac this same vowel + s suffix can also be used for the dubiative if the rising intonation, which characterizes the interrogative, is omitted (See Delisle 1976 pg.114 where the information is said to come from Don Dublois.

		Affirmative	**Negative**
1	sing.	nωwadchanumun	nωwadchanumunás
2	sing.	kωwadchanumun	kωwadchanumunás
3	sing.	ωwadchanumun	ωwadchanumunáous
1	pl. e.	nωwadchanumumun	nωwadchanumunnanonus
1	pl. i.		
2	pl.	kωwadchanumumwω	kωwadchanumunnáous
3	pl.	wadchanumwog	ωwadchanumunnáous

The N. -*as* corresponds with the Blackfoot suffix -*ats*(-*p*-*ats*), which is used in the same manner, e.g., *kit-ai-tappo(p)ats* 'are you (sing.) going there?': *kit-ai-tappo* 'you (sing.) go there'. Often the prefix *kŭttai*-, which is placed after the pronominal prefix, is used simultaneously, e.g., *ki-kŭttai-tappo(p)ats*= *kit-ai-tappo(p)ats*. One also affixes the suffix -*ats* to the negative verbal forms if they are employed interrogatively, but -*stai* then serves exclusively as a negative prefix, e.g., *kit-ak-stai-tappo(p)ats* 'shall you (sing.) not go there?', *kit-ak-stai-otsipats* 'shall you (sing.) not take it?'.

§ 39. A portion of the **dubiative** forms in Ojibway is characterized by the syllable -*dog*(-), to which the Cree -*toke* or -*tuke* corresponds.[49] Examples: O. *nind-ikkitomidog* 'perhaps I say', *ikkito(wi)dog* 'perhaps he says', *kawin nind-ikkitosimidog* 'perhaps I say not'; C. *ni-inipānātoke* 'perhaps I sleep', *nipātoke* 'perhaps he sleeps'. In general, there is all sorts of agreement between the dubiative conjugation of Ojibway and Cree as well as concerning forms that do not contain the mentioned suffix. The suffix -*en*, which we find in Ojibway for the dubiative conjuctive, turns up again in Cree as -*e*, e.g., O. *degwišinowānen* 'If I perhaps arrive', *degwišinowanen* 'If you (sing.) perhaps arrive', *degwišinogwen* 'If he perhaps arrives': *dagwišin* 'he arrives'; C. *nepāwāne* 'If I perhaps sleep'. *nepāwane* 'if you (sing.) perhaps sleep', *nepākwe* 'If he perhaps sleeps': *nipaw*

---

49. cf. M. *etuk* 'probably' Dawe 1986 and see below under Micmac.

'he sleeps'. One sees, that the dubiative conjunctive forms exhibit mutated vocalism.

I am leaving out the various degrees of probability, which Cree expresses in the system of the dubiative conjugation.[50]

---

50. Micmac may have as many as three or more historic dubiatives one of which is mentioned in § 38 with the interrogatives. Father Pacifique gives *etuk* and *jiptuk* 'perhaps' as the particles with which the dubiative is formed, but about the forms he says that "they are not very numerous" (perhaps indicating that these forms were in the process of being phased out) and that one could use *etuk* and *jiptuk* as adverbs without incorporating them into the verb H&F 1990. A means of indicating the dubiative that is given by Dawe is given below (V indicates the presence of a stem final vowel.).

		Dubiative			Preterite Alterations		
		AI	TI	psTI	AI	TI	psTI
1	sing.	-Vyas	-map	-ap		ə	ə
2	sing.	-Vsap	-musap	-usap	t		
3	sing.	-Vs	-akas	-oqos			
1	dual excl.	-Veksap	-meksap	-ueksap			
1	dual incl.	-Vyikus	-mukus	-tukus			
2	dual	-Vyoqsap	-moqsap	-uoqsap	o	o	o
3	dual	-Vsanik	-ksanik	-oqosanik			
1	pl. excl.	-V(l)tiyeksap	-mu:tiyeksap	-u:tiyeksap	a		
1	pl. incl.	-V(l)ti:kus	-mu:tiyukus	-u:tikus			
2	pl.	-V(l)tiyoqsap	-mu:tiyoqsap	-u:tiyoqsap	o	o	o
3	pl.	-V(l)tisanik	-mu:ti:tisanik	-u:tisanik			

		TA				
		Dubiative		Preterite	
		Direct	Inverse	Direct	Inverse
1	sing.	(-(V)ks p),[-(V)q s]	-is	-(V)kap	-ip
2	sing.	-(V)sap,(-(V)ts p)	-(V)skas	-(V)tap	-(V)skap
3	sing.	-asnl,(-asnn)	-asnl	-apnl (apnn)	(-atapnn),[-apenl]
1	pl. excl.	-(V)kas	-inamtsap	-(V)kap (-(V)katap)	(-inamtap)
1	pl. incl.	-V)kus	-ulkus,(-ulksap)	-(V)kup	(-alkap),[-ulkop]
2	pl.	-oqos	-uloqos, (-oqsap)	-oqop	-uloqop, (-noqop)
3	pl.	-a:tisanel	(-ukwi:tisapnn) or [ukwi:tisnn]	-a:tipnl	-ukwi:tip or (-ukwi:tipnn)

The dubiative prefix in Blackfoot is completely different, as will become readily apparent from the following examples: *nŏks-ka-kŭm-ŭkometŭkki* 'perhaps I love': *nit-ŭkometŭkki* 'I love', *kŏks-ka-kŭm-ŭkometŭkki* 'perhaps you (sing.) love' *kit-ŭkometŭkki* 'you (sing.) love', *nŏks-ka-kŭm-oka* 'perhaps I sleep': *nit-ai-oka* 'I sleep': *ŏks-ka-kŭm-okau* 'perhaps he sleeps': *ai-okau* 'he sleeps', *nŏks-ka-kŭm-sau-oka* 'perhaps I sleep not': *ni-mat-ai-okapa* 'I sleep not', *i-kŭm-i-okainiki* 'if I perhaps sleep': *okainiki* 'if I sleep', *maks-i-kŭm-i-okainiki* 'if I shall perhaps sleep': *mak-okainiki* 'if I shall sleep'.

§ 40. When we proceed to the actual modes, the **indicative** comes up first for discussion.

For examples of the intransitive conjugation with animate subject I choose O. *nin-nibā*, C. *ni-nipān* 'I sleep', M. *nil ygaye* 'I strike', N. *nωwaantam* 'I am wise', B. *nit-ŭkometŭkki* 'I love'.

		TA Dubitative		Preterite	
		Direct	Inverse	Direct	Inverse
2	acting on 1.	-isəp	[-uləs]	-itəp	-ulep
2	(or 3) on 1 pl.e.	-iekəs	-ulekəs	-iek p	-ulekəp
2	pl. on 1.	-ioqos	[-uloqos]	-ioqop	(-uloqop)

The forms for the AI, TI and psTI are nearly identical to the preterite forms. So much so in fact that if you drop the *s* completely and replace it with a *p* if there is not already one present in the form and then drop the underlined letters and replace them with the Preterite alterations where indicated you are left with the preterite form (in these tables above *p* is in no case underlined. The first person singulars of the TI and the ps TI are irregular and do not contain the *s*. These preterite forms are *-map* and *-ap* respectively. The Abreviation ps TI stands for pseudo-transitive inanimate verbs, Bloomfield says this "About half the tr. an. verbs are matched not by tr. inan. verbs but by pseudo-transitive verbs, namely intr. verbs formed mostly with the suffixes *-too, -htoo* and taking implied objects." (Bloomfield 1946:95). The TA forms are far more complicated and for this reason the preterite forms have been given in full. In all cases except the bottom three the Direct indicates action on a third person and the inverse indicates action by a third person. In the same way, for the bottom three forms, the inverse indicates the reversal of the direction of the action. Round brackets in the above table indicate forms collected from a native speaker and these forms include dialectical variants. The forms in square brackets have been reconstructed based on the other given forms. This information and these tables have been drawn from Dawe 1986.

		O.	**C.**
1	sing.	*nin-nibā*	*ni-nipān*
2	sing.	*ki-nibā*	*ki-nipān*
3	sing.	*nibā*	*nipaw*
1	pl. e.	*nin-nibāmin*	*ni-nipānān*
1	pl. i.	*ki-nibāmin*	*ki-nipān(ān)ow*
2	pl.	*ki-nibām*	*ki-nipānāwaw*
3	pl.	*nibāwag*	*nipāwok*

		M.	**N.**
1	sing.	*nil ygaye*	*nωwaantam*
2	sing.	*kil ygan*	*kωwaantam*
3	sing.	*negeum ygat*	*waantamnoh*
1	pl. e.	*ninen ygayek*	*nωwaantamumun*
1	pl. i.	*kinu ygayku*	
2	pl.	*kilau ygayok*	*kωwaantamumwω*
3	pl.	*negmau ygagik*	*waantamwog*

[47]

		B.
1	sing.	*nit-ŭkometŭkki*
2	sing.	*kit-ŭkometŭkki*
3	sing.	*ŭkometŭkkiu*
1	pl. e.	*nit-ŭkometŭkkipinan*
1	pl. i.	*ŭkometŭkkiop*
2	pl.	*kit-ŭkometŭkkipuau*
3	pl.	*ŭkometŭkkiau*

The comparison of Ojibway with Natick and Blackfoot makes it probable that the first two persons of the singular had no suffix in Proto-Algonquian and that the forms of Cree are less archaic in this case. Still, this must go back to the time when Ojibway and Cree had not yet seperated from each other, for the *n* of Cree appears in the imperfect of Ojibway (*nin-nibānaban, ki-nibānaban*). Thus, in that period, equivalent forms with and without *n*, must have existed next to each other. The third person singular must have had a final *u* or *w* for a portion of the intransitive verbs, since the agreement of C. *nipaw* and B. *ŭkometŭkkiu* cannot be well explained otherwise. I am speaking only of a portion of the intransitive verbs, since not all of the subdivisions of this class in Blackfoot, have *-u* as the third person inflection. As appears from Ojibway, Cree and Natick the third person plural terminated in *-wak* or something similar to it. The comparison of the intransitive paradigms also instructs us that the third person, in contrast to the first and second person, had no pronominal prefix in this language family. More over, there are particular agreements to be noted such as: O. *nin-nibāmin*: N. *nωwaantamumun*, C. *ni-nipānān*: B. *nit-ŭkometŭkkipinan*, C. *ki-nipānawaw*: N. *kωwaantamumwω*: *kit-ŭkometŭkkipuau* . Micmac has completely deviated from the original schemes.

Leaving out the uni-personals, the basics whereof can already be found in § 33 if necessary, I now turn to the transitive verb with animate object. My examples are: O. *nin-wābama* 'I see him', C. *ni-mowaw* 'I eat him', N. *nωwadchan* 'I keep him', B. *nit-ŭkomĭmmau* 'I love him'. I have no suitable paradigms for Micmac. [48]

		O.	**C.**
1	sing.	nin-wābama	ni-mowaw
2	sing.	ki-wābama	ki-mowaw
3	sing.	o-wābamān	mowew
1	pl. e.	nin-wābamānān	ni-mowānān
1	pl. i.	ki-wābamānān	ki-mowān(ān)ow
2	pl.	ki-wābamāwa	ki-mowāwaw

		O.	**C.**
3	pl.	owābamāwan	mowewok

		N.	**B.**
1	sing.	nωwadchan	nit-ŭkomĭmmau
2	sing.	kωwadchan	kit-ŭkomĭmmau
3	sing.	ωwadchanuh	nit-ŭkomĭmmiuaie
1	pl. e.	nωwadchanoun	nit-ŭkomĭmmŭnan
1	pl. i.		
2	pl.	kωwadchanau	kit-ŭkomĭmmauau
3	pl.	ωwadchanouh	ŭkomĭmmiauaie

[J.S.: see footnotes.⁵¹, ⁵²]

51.

		Micmac TA from Proulx	**From Dawe:** *pema'lĭk* 'to carry'
1	sg.	tax'mĭk 'I hit him'	pema'lĭk
2	sg.	tax'mĭt 'thou hittest him'	pema'lĭt
3	sg.	tax'mat'l 'he hits him'	pema'lajl
1	pl. e.	tax'mĭkĭt 'we hit him'	pema'lĭkĭt
1	pl. i.	tax'mu:k 'we hit him'	pema'lu'kw
2	pl.	tax'mox 'ye hit him'	pema'loq
3	pl.	tax'ma:tit'l 'they hit him'	pema'la'tijl

52. Here the Micmac forms for this mode have developed out of the Conjunct (compare with TA Conjunct forms below from the other languages). The -*l* occurring in the third persons is the regular obviative added to the historical Conjunct. As can be seen in the forms from Dawe, the -*t*- preceding this obviative suffix, is sometimes -*j*-. With regards to the Unchanged and Changed Conjunct Dawe says this concerning the Independent, pg. 186 "The stem contraction of the unchanged forms distinguishes them from the independent forms while the changed conjunct forms are distinguished from the independent forms by thier use or sentential context".

Although points of agreement are not absent between the various languages, as yet it is not possible to restore the proto-Algonquian paradigm. The first two persons probably both had the termination *u* or *w* in the singular, which has fallen away in Ojibway. The Natick forms *nωwadchan* and *kωwadchan* differ completely. N. *ωwadchanuh* in contrast, compares with O. *o-wābamān*. The identity of the terminations in the first person exclusives and in the second person plural (-apart from N. *kωwadchanau*-) is obvious.

If we compare these transitive forms with the intransitive forms just mentioned we get the impression that the intransitive plural is influenced by the transitive here and there, but it would be premature to wish to have this demonstrated in any detail already. Let us wait until we have extensive material of a great number of languages at our disposal.

I have only given paradigms for forms of the intransitive and the transitive with singular animate third-person-object, but also the comparison of other form ranges —with plural animate third-person's-object, with first- and second-person-objects - should undoubtedly yield some results. Here however I will only give the framework of a comparative grammar,{i} an outline that can be filled in later. One finds examples of the one and then the other (also from the reflexive of the sub-ordinated third person in the verbal form) in § 49. where the incorporation is treated. It is fitting to my task here to impart the paradigms of the transitive verb with inanimate object, whereby I shall again limit myself to the case in which this object is singular. I choose as examples: O. *nin-wābandān* 'I see it', C. *ni-mitšin* 'I eat it', M. *šaktem* 'I obey it', N. *nωwadchanumun* 'I keep it', B. *nit-ŭkometsip* 'I love it'.

[49]

		O.	C.
1	sing.	nin-wābandān	ni-mitšin
2	sing.	ki-wābandān	ki-mitšin
3	sing.	o-wābandān	mitšiw
1	pl. e.	nin-wābandāmin	ni-mitšinān
1	pl. i.	ki-wābandāmin	ki-mitšin(ān)ow
2	pl.	ki-wābandānawa	ni-mitšināwaw

		O.	**C.**
3	pl.	o-wābandānawa	mitšiwok

		M.	**N.**
1	sing.	šaktem	nωwadchanumun
2	sing.	šaktemen	kωwadchanumun
3	sing.	šaktek	ωwadchanumun
1	pl. e.	šaktemutiek	nωwadchanumumun
1	pl. i.	šaktemutiku	
2	pl.	šaktemutiok	kωwadchanumumwω
3	pl.	šaktemutitiš	wadchanumwog

		B.
1	sing.	nit-ŭkometsip
2	sing.	kit-ŭkometsip
3	sing.	ŭkometsĭmaie
1	pl. e.	nit-ŭkometsipinan
1	pl. i.	ŭkometsip
2	pl.	kit-ŭkometsipuau
3	pl.	ŭkometsimiau

It is noteworthy that in Cree the *ni-mitšin* paradigm agrees completely with the intransitive *ni-nipān*. There are also points of agreement in the other dialects, especially in Micmac, but nowhere does the similarity go so far as in Cree. Ojibway, which is archaic in many other aspects, has also best maintained the intransitive and both of the transitive conjugations.

In Micmac there are also dual forms, but these I omit, unless, for one reason or another it is desirable to mention them.

§ 41. I now give examples of the **conjunctive**, which also exhibits a quite large diversity of personal terminations. Except in Micmac and in Blackfoot the pronominal prefixes are generally missing.

For the intransitive conjugation with animate subject I take O. *ikkitoiān* 'if I say, that I say', C. *nipāyān* 'if I sleep, that I sleep'. M. *ntamalkan* 'that I dance', N. *waantamon* 'if I am wise', B. *nŏk-ŭkometŭksi* 'that I love'.

		O.	C.
1	sing.	ikkitoiān	nipāyān
2	sing.	ikkitoian	nipāyan
3	sing.	ikkitod	nipāt
1	pl. e.	ikkitoiāng	nipāyāk
1	pl. i.	ikkitoiang	nipāyak
2	pl.	ikkitoieg	nipāyek
3	pl.	ikkitowad	nipātšik (nipātwaw)

		M.	N.
1	sing.	ntamalkan	waantamon
2	sing.	ktamalkan	waantaman
3	sing.	uftamalkan	waantog
1	pl. e.	ntamalkanen	waantamog
1	pl. i.	ktamalkanenu	
2	pl.	ktamalkanau	waantamóg
3	pl.	uftamalkanau	waantamohettit

		B.
1	sing.	nŏk-ŭkometŭksi
2	sing.	kŏk-ŭkometŭksi

		B.
3	sing.	mŏk-ŭkometŭksi
1	pl. e.	nŏk-ŭkometŭksinan
1	pl. i.	ŏk-ŭkometŭkiosi
2	pl.	kŏk-ŭkometŭksuau
3	pl.	mŏk-ŭkometŭkĭsau

[J.S.: see footnote.[53]]

[51]   The close relationship of Ojibway and Cree, especially in the singular, immediately catches the eye. Concerning Micmac, which may be lacking the pronouns in the indicative, the presence of inseperable prefixes in the conjunctive is surprising.[54]

---

53. Mi'kmaq Conjunct vs Subordinative

		Endings from Dawe		
		Unchanged		Changed
	H&F 1990	AI	II	II
Alasutmay 'to pray'				
1	alasutma 'n	-Vyan		
2	alasutman	-Vn		
3	alasutmaj	-Vč	-Vk	-Vk
1 d. e.	alasutmayek	-Vyek		
1 d. i.	alasutmayikw	-Vyikw		
2 d.	alasutmayoq	-Vyoq		
3 d.	alasutma'tij	-V:tič	-Vs	-Vk
1 pl. e.	alasutma'tiyek	-Vtiyek		
1 pl. i.	alasutma'ti'kw	-Vti:kw		
2 pl.	alsutma'tiyoq	-Vtiyoq		
3 pl.	alsutma'ti'tij	-Vti:tič	-Vs an	-Vtik

54. What Uhlenbeck is actually providing here for Mi'kmaq, is the subordinative, and it can be seen from the actual conjunct of the verb *alsutmay* from H&F 1990 and the endings of this conjugation taken from Dawe, that there do appear to be striking similarities, especially with Cree and Ojibway. The main difference in the plural form of Mi'kmaq is an additional -*ti*- infix, which is an innovation that distinguishes the plural forms from the dual forms (these dual forms are derived from the historical plural, and they are quite similar to the plurals of Cree and Ojibway.

Blackfoot has a completely variant formation in which the personal prefixes, of which the *m-* in the third person is not related to the independent pronoun, are connected to the inseparable prefix *ok-*. This prefix is in certain cases *ŏks* (eg. *nŏks-okasi*; that I might sleep'), of which forms we have already come to know in § 39.

For examples of the transitive conjugation with animate object I choose O. *wābamag* 'if I see him, that I see him', C. *mowak* 'if I eat him, that I eat him'. N. *wadchanog* 'if I keep him'. B. *nŏkŭkomĭmmosi* 'that I might love him'. I have no suitable paradigms for Micmac.

		O.	C.
1	sing.	wābamag	mowak
2	sing.	wābamad	mowat
3	sing.	wābamād	mowāt

Concerning the subordinative Dawe says "The subordinative is the only verbal paradigm in Micmac which has personal prefixes throughout.", but Proulx says that Newfoundland dialect uses prefixes while the other dialects do not. Dawe also says "...in Modern Micmac these prefixes are becoming lost."

On the surface the subordinative gives the appearance of being similar to the conjunct in function as it is regularly translated as 'that I dance etc.' See H&F 1990 for example. The only commentary I could find on the function of the subordinative is from Dawe where she quotes Goddard. "The subordinative mode "...is used for the verb of sentential complements in certain constructions."(Goddard 1983:351)".

Concerning the Cojunct Dawe says this: "There are two forms of the conjunct: the changed conjunct which is used in "when-clauses" and the unchanged conjunct which is used in "if-clauses". The unchanged conjunct does not have any initial change and is therefore contracted (ex. pmiej) whereas the changed conjunct does have initial change and is consequently uncontracted (ex. pemiej).

With regards to the contracted vs. uncontracted stem there is an observation to be made. The unchanged conjunct like the future and imperative refers to possible events. These three tenses (and modes) all involve contracted stems. The changed conjunct refers to real events and does not involve a contraction. It seems that there is a relation between whether an event is possible or real and whether the stem is contracted or not."

Dawe also says "These conjunct endings are very similar to the endings of the independent indicative present. The contraction, which occurs in the unchanged forms is what distinguishes them from the independent forms. The forms of the changed conjunct are very similar to those of the independent with regards to both the stem and the inflections and thus these forms are to be distinguished from each other by their use (their sentential context)."

		O.	**C.**
1	pl. e.	wābamangid	mowakit
1	pl. i.	ki-wābamang	mowak
2	pl.	ki-wābameg	mowek
3	pl.	wābamawad	mowātšik (mowātwaw)

		N.	**B.**
1	sing.	wadchanog	nŏk-ŭkomĭmmŏsi
2	sing.	wadchanadt	kŏk-ŭkomĭmmŏsi
3	sing.	wadchanont	mŏk-ŭkomĭmmŏsi
1	pl. e.	wadchanogkut	nŏk-ŭkomĭmmŏsinan
1	pl. i.		
2	pl.	wadchanóg	kŏk-ŭkomĭmmŏsau
3	pl.	wadchanukáhettit	mŏk-ŭkomĭmmŏsauaie

[J.S.: see footnote.⁵⁵]

The relationship of Ojibway and Cree, to which Natick also corresponds, is quite close. Blackfoot again occupies a separate place with its ŏk- and -si.

55.

		Micmac TA Conjunct from H&F1990	Endings from Dawe "( )" indicates no vowel in some verbs. "V" indicates vowel variation
1	sing.	nmi'k 'if I see him'	-(V)k
2	sing.	nmi'j 'if you see him'	-(V)č
3	sing.	nmiaj 'if he sees him'	-ač
1	pl.e.	nmi'kîj 'if we see him'	-(V)keč
1	pl.i.	nmi'kw 'if we see him' {j}	-(V)kw
2	pl.	nmioq 'if ye see him'	-oq
3	pl.	nmia'tij 'if they see him'	-a:tič

O. *wābandāmān* 'if I see it, that I see it', C. *mitšiyān* 'if I eat it, that I eat it', M. *nšaktemen* 'that I might obey it', N. *wadchanumon* 'If I keep it', B. *nŏk-ŭkometsĭssi* 'that I love it', serve as examples for the transitive conjugation with inanimate object. [52]

		O.	C.
1	sing.	wābandāmān	mitšiyān
2	sing.	wābandāman	mitšiyan
3	sing.	wābandāng	mitšit
1	pl. e.	wābandāmāng	mitšiyāk
1	pl. i.	wābandāmang	mitšiyak
2	pl.	wābandāmeg	mitšiyek
3	pl.	wābandāmowad	mitšitšik

		M.	N.
1	sing.	nšaktemen	wadchanumon
2	sing.	kšaktemen	wadchanuman
3	sing.	ušaktemen	wadchanuk
1	pl. e.	nšaktemutinen	wadchanumog
1	pl. i.	kšaktemutinenu	
2	pl.	kšaktemutinau	wadchanumóg
3	pl.	uškedemutinau	wadchanumahettit

		B.
1	sing.	nŏk-ŭkometsĭssi
2	sing.	kŏk-ŭkometsĭssi
3	sing.	mŏk-ŭkometsĭssi
1	pl. e.	nŏk-ŭkometsĭsinan

		B.
1	pl. i.	ŏk-ŭkometsĭssi
2	pl.	kŏk-ŭkometsĭssuai
3	pl.	mŏk-ŭkometsĭssauaie

[J.S.: See footnote.[56]]

56.

		H&F 1990 **TI**	**Endings from Dawe** **TI**
	nestm 'to understand'		
1		nsîtman	-man
2		nsîtmn	-mn
3		nsîj	-ək
1	d. e.	nsîtmek	-mek
1	d. i.	nsîtmu'kw	-mu:kw
2	d.	nsîtmoq	-moq
3	d.	nsîtmi'tij	-mi:tič
1	pl. e.	nsîtmu'tiyek	-mu:tiyek
1	pl. i.	nsîtmu'ti'kw	-mu:ti:kw
2	pl.	nsîtmu'tiyok	-mu:tiyoq
3	pl.	nsîtmu'ti'tij	-mu:ti:tič
		H&F 1990 **psTI**	**Endings from Dawe**
mena'tu 'to remove, to tear out'			
1	sing.	mna'tuan	-uan
2	sing.	mna'tu'n	-un
3	sing.	mna'toq	-oq
1	d. e.	mna'tuek	-uek
1	d. i.	mna'tu'kw	-u:kw
2	d.	mna'toq	-uoq
3	d.	mna'tu'tij	-u:tič
1	pl. e.	mna'tu'tiyek	-utiyek
1	pl. i.	mna'tuti'kw	-u:ti:kw
2	pl.	mna'tu'tiyok	-u:tiyoq

The same, which applies to the paradigms of the intransitive, also applies to these paradigms, the actual personal endings of which vary only slightly. I do not need to bring up the existing differences because they can be summed up in a single glance. M. *uškedmutinau* is peculiar- but not on account of the ending-, which connects however in its peculiarity, to some other forms of *šaktem*.

Ojibway and Cree also have an **iterative conjunct**, which is derived from the common conjunct by mutation of the first vowel and simultaneous suffixing of O. *-in*, C. *-i*, e.g., O. *ekkitoiānin* 'every time when I say', C. *nipāyāni* 'every time when I sleep'. The *d* of the third person singular and plural in Ojibway becomes *dž* before *i* (*ekkitodžin, ekkitowadžin*).[57]

The **personal gerunds** of Ojibway and Cree, which are not char- [53] acterized by any suffix, but only by mutation, are also based on the conjunctive. The only exception to this general rule is the third person plural in Ojibway, which is formed by suffixing of *-ig* to the third person singular. Just as in the iterative conjunctive, before *i*, *d* becomes *dž*. In Cree, the third person plural of the conjunctive has the same gutteral suffixes as those of the personal gerund. I have already stated examples of the personal gerunds in the treatment of the mutation under § 31. For clarity here I contrast the Ojibway -paradigms for *nin ekkitoiān* 'I who say' and *ikkitoiān* 'if I say, that I say'.

		Personal gerund.	**Conjunctive.**
1	sing.	*nin ekkitoiān*	*ikkitoiān*
2	sing.	*kin ekkitoian*	*ikkitoian*

		H&F 1990 psTI	Endings from Dawe
3	pl.	*mna'tu'ti'tij*	*-uːtiːtič*

Above Uhlenbeck gives the subordinative and I am supplying the actual conjunct below it. The endings of the unchanged conjunct and the changed conjunct are the same

57. According to Proulx Mi'kmaq has the iterative Suffix *-el* which appears to be the same morpheme as the *-l* given for the 'when' conjuct in H&F 1990. According to Proulx "a verb in the itterative tense is accompanied by the particle *ekel* 'every so often' or *teːs-ekel* 'every time' in the same sentence."

		Personal gerund.	**Conjunctive.**
3	sing.	win ekkitod	ikkitod
1	pl. e.	ninawind ekkitoiāng	ikkitoiāng
1	pl. i.	kinawind ekkitoiang	ikkitoiang
2	pl.	kinawa ekkitoieg	ikkitoieg
3	pl.	winawa ekkitodžig	ikkitowad

Micmac also has personal gerunds, but only the first and second person singular belong to the conjunctive system. From *amalkānel* 'I that dance', and *amalkanek* 'when I danced', the conjunctive character appears immediately from the *n* (*ntamalkan* 'that I may dance'), but for *amalkǎnel* 'you (sing.) dancing' and *amalkanek* 'when you (sing.) danced', one could occassionaly hesitate a moment as to whether they should be compared with the indicative *amalkan* rather than with the conjunctive *ktamalkan*. The difference in quantity that exists between *amalkānel* and *amalkǎnel*, makes us nevertheless expect that the second person form is also conjunctive and that the relationship of *amalkānel* to *amalkǎnel* is the same for example, as that of O. *ekkitoiān* to *ekkitoian*. It is unfortunate that the paradigms of the verbal classes of Micmac cannot raise beyond all doubt, the mentioned difference in quantity. Apart from the first and second person singular, the personal gerunds of Micmac are derived from the indicative.

In contrast to Ojibway for example, tense indicating and suppositional subordinate clauses are not conveyed by the conjunctive in Blackfoot, but by separate forms, of which only a few are related to the conjunctive. Examples of this mode, which for the time being, I will indicate as the second conjunctive, are:

- *okainiki* 'if I sleep, if you (sing.) sleep',
- *okasi* 'if he sleeps' (:*mŏks-okasi* 'that he might sleep).
- *ŭkomĭmmŭnaniki* 'if we love him',
- *ŭkomĭmŭsaie* 'if he loves him' (:*mŏk-ŭkomĭmmŏsi* 'that he might love him').
- *ŭkometsĭmenoainiki* 'if you (plur.) love it'.
- *ŭkometsĭssi* 'if he loves it' (:*mŏk-ŭkometsĭssi* 'that he might love it').

One can see that the characteristic element *-niki* is absent in the third person forms.

§ 42. In Ojibway and Cree, the optative is formed from the indicative by means of the prefix *wi-* (mutated *wā-*). A few examples from Ojibway should be sufficient:

- *nin-wi-nibā* 'I want to sleep, I wish to sleep'.
- *ki-wi-nōndāgo* 'you (sing.) wish to be heard'.
- *o-wi-wābandānsin* 'he does not want to see it'.
- *wā-ižād* 'he who wants to go'.
- *wā-anamiādžig* 'they who wish to pray'.

In Natick, the optative is usually characterized by peculiar personal suffixes with the additional suffix *-toh* and more over by vowel lengthening in the first syllable. I will give some paradigms of the optative beside the corresponding tables of the indicative to better contrast the differences. My examples are: *nωwáaantamuh-toh* 'I want to be wise',: *nωwaantam* 'I am wise', *nωwaadchanun-toh* 'I want to keep him',: *nωwadchan* 'I keep him', *nωwáadchánumun-toh* 'I want to keep it',: *nωwadchanumun* 'I keep it'.

		Indicative.	**Optative.**
1	sing.	nωwaantam	nωwáaantamun-toh
2	sing.	kωwaantam	kωwáaantamun-toh
3	sing.	waantamnoh	ωwáaantamun-toh
1	pl. e.	nωwaantamumun	nωwáaantamuman-toh
1	pl. i.		
2	pl.	kωwaantamumwω	kωwáaantamuneau-toh
3	pl.	waantamωog	ωwáaantamuneau-toh

[55]

		Indicative.	Optative.
1	sing.	nωwadchan	nωwaadchanun-toh
2	sing.	kωwadchan	kωwaadchanon-toh
3	sing.	ωwadchanuh	ωwaadchanon-toh
1	pl. e.	nωwadchanoun	nωwaadchanonan-toh
1	pl. i.		
2	pl.	kωwadchanau	kωwaadchanóneau-toh
3	pl.	ωwadchanouh	ωwaadchanóneau-toh

		Indicative.	Optative.
1	sing.	nωwadchanumun	nωwáadchánumun-toh
2	sing.	kωwadchanumun	kωwáadchanumun-toh
3	sing.	ωwadchanumun	ωwaadchanumun-toh
1	pl. e.	nωwadchanumumun	nωwaadchanumunnan-toh
1	pl. i.		
2	pl.	kωwadchanumumwω	kωwadchanumunnan-toh
3	pl.	wadchanumwog	ωwadchanumuneau-toh

§ 43. In some languages we find a **potential**. The potential of Cree has the prefix *gi-*(*ki-*) as a distinguishing mark. e.g., *ni-gi-toten* 'I can do it'.[58]

---

58. The following are some of the forms for the Potential in Mi'kmaq. There is also an attestive mode and many aspects of directionality I must omit here for the sake of brevity, and practicality. It would seem that verb stems, which end in a consonant, begin the Potential suffix with a vowel (-*a* for TA and -*u* for AI), but if they end in a vowel this part of the suffix is omitted. For comparison I am providing the AI forms as well. All forms here are from Proulx.

		TA	
1	sing.	s'max	'I coud feed him/them' (alternate form in *s'miyek*)

In Blackfoot, we find two differing formations the first of which is characterized by the prefix *kot(s)*, the second by the prefix *ŭskak(s)-*.

Examples of *kot(s)*:

- *nit-o-kot-ŭkometŭkki* 'I am capable of loving'.
- *i-kot-ŭkometŭkkiu* 'he is capable of loving'.
- *nit-o-kots-oka* 'I am ready to sleep'.
- *i-kots-okau* 'he is ready to sleep'.
- *nit-o-kot-ŭkomĭmmau* 'I am capable of loving him'.
- *i-kot-ŭkomĭmmiuaie* 'he is capable of loving him'.
- *nit-o-kot-ŭkometsip* 'I am capable of loving it'.
- *i-kot-ŭkometsĭmiau* 'he is capable of loving it'.

Examples of *ŭskak(s)-*:

- *ŭskak-ŭkometŭkkiu* 'He can love'.
- *nit-ŭskaks-oka* 'I can sleep'.
- *kit-ŭskak-ŭkomĭmmau* 'you (sing.) can love him'.
- *ŭskak-ŭkometsimiau* 'they can love it'.

		TA	
2	sing.	s'max	'you could feed him/them'
3	sing.	s'mas	'he could feed him/them'
1	pl. e.	s'maxek	'we could feed him/them'
1	pl. i.	s'ma:xop	'we could feed him/them'
2	pl.	s'maxox	'ye could feed him/them'
3	pl.	s'ma:tis	'they could feed him/them'
		AI	
1	sing.	ktukwi:muk	'I could run'
2	sing.	ktukwi:muk	'you could run'
3	sing.	ktukwi:-s	'he could run'
1	pl. e.	ktukwi:mukek	'we could run'
1	pl. i.	ktukwi:mukup	'we could run'
2	pl.	ktuwi:mukox	'ye could run'
3	pl.	ktukwi:mi:tis	'they could run'

Additionaly there is a II sufix *-N-s msîki:ktîs* 'it/they(inan.) would be big'

§ 44. The **conditional** is characterized by the prefix *da-* in Ojibway, and *pa-* in Cree.

Examples in Ojibway:

- *nin-da-ikkit* 'I would say'.
- *nin-da-gi-ikkit* 'I would have said'.
- *ki-da-wābamāwa* 'you (sing.) would see him'.
- *o-da-wābamigowan* 'they would have seen'.
- *ki-da-pakitēom* 'you (sing.) would strike me'.
- *nin-da-minikwēmin* 'we would drink it'.

The prefix *pa-* in Cree occurs in exactly the same way as that of *da-* in Ojibway, so examples are unnecessary.

In contrast we find a conditional with peculiar personal endings in Micmac. As examples I give *amalkag* 'I would dance' and *šaktemuk* 'I would obey it'.

1	sing.	amalkag	šaktemuk
2	sing.	amalkakp	šaktemukp
3	sing.	amalkaš	škets
1	du. e.	amalkagekp	šaktemugep
1	du. i.	amalkakup	šaktemukup
2	du.	amalkakog	šaktemugokp
3	du.	amalkatiš	šaktemitiš
1	pl. e.	amalkaldigekp	šaktemutigekp
1	pl. i.	amalkaldikup	šaktemutikup
2	pl.	amalkaldigokp	šaktemutigokp
3	pl.	amlakalditiš	šaktemutitiš

[J.S.: See footnote.[59]]

---

59. Concerning the *-p* ending given here by Uhlenbeck in the second person singular and the exclusive first person dual and plural, I have not been able to find another source giving this ending and Dawe does not mention it in her historical derivation. Below are forms taken from Dawe.

§ 45. Of the modes, the **imperitive** still has to be discussed.

		AI	II	TI	psTI	TA
1	sing.	-Vk		-muk	-uk	-iek
2	sing.	-Vk		-muk	-uk	-aq
3	sing.	-Vs	-Vs	-s	-s	-as
1	du. e.	-Vkek		-mukek	-ukek	
1	du. i.	-V:kup		-mukup	-ukup	
2	du.	-Vkoq		-mokoq	-ukoq	
3	du.	-V:tis		-mi:tis	-u:tis	
1	pl. e.	-Vtikek		-mu:tikek	-u:tikek	-aqek
1	pl. i.	-Vtikup		-mu:tikup	-u:tikup	-aqup
2	pl.	-Vtikoq		-mu:tikoq	-u:tikoq	-aqoq
3	pl.	-Vti:tis		-mu:titis	-u:titis	-a:tis

The Transitive animate has no dual forms. As has been stated elsewhere, the dual is really the historical plural and the forms still function as such in the TA forms. There are other forms for the TA verbs, but they are not for action on a third person. Dawe Suggests that the conditional of Micmac is related to what is known as the delayed imperative in Plains Cree and Eastern Ojibway. Concerning the similarity in meaning she says this. "The Micmac conditional refers to actions conditioned by something else while the delayed imperative commands for action after an intervening event." The limited forms compared there are given below. As these forms are imperative they only have forms addressing the second person.

	Plains Cree	Eastern Ojibway	Micmac
	AI		
sg. 1	-hkan	-kkan	-Vk
pl.1 (i)	-hkek		-V:kup
pl.2	-hkahk		-V:koq
	TI		
sg. 1 (noted as 2 in Dawe)	-amo:hkan	-kkan	-muk
pl.1 (i) (noted as 21 in Dawe)	-amo:hkahk		-mokup
pl.2 (noted as 22 in Dawe)	-amo:hkek		-mokoq

Ojibway examples from Valentine are *bi-zhaakan* '(you sg.) come later', *biidookan* '(you sg.) bring it later' and *wiindmawshikan* '(you sg.) tell me about it later'. All of these examples occur in a sentence that also contains the word *baamaa* 'later'.

Concerning the following paradigms, it should be mentioned in advance that the first person plur. in C. -k(ak), the second person sing. in O. and C. -kan, and the second person plur. in O. -keg and C. -kek are considered to be future imperitive.

O. *ikkiton* 'say', C. *nipa* 'sleep', M. *amalka* 'dance', N. *waantash* 'to be wise', and B. *okat* 'sleep' serve as examples of the intransitive conjugation with an animate subject.

		O.	C.
2	sing.	*ikkiton, ikkitokan*	*nipa, nipākan*
3	sing.	*ta-ikkito*	*kata-nipaw*
1	pl. e.	*ikkitoda*	*nipātaw, nipātān, nipātāk, nipāk, nipākak*
1	pl. i.		
2	pl.	*ikkitog ikkitoiog ikkitokeg*	*nipāk, nipākek*
3	pl.	*ta-ikkitowag*	*kata-nipāwok*

[57]

		M.	N.
2	sing.	*amalka*	*waantash*
3	sing.	*amalkaš*	*waantaj*
1	du. e.	*amalkaneš*	
1	du. i.		
2	du.	*amalkak*	
3	du.	*amalkaiš*	
1	pl. e.	*amalkaldineš*	*waantamuttuh*
1	pl. i.		
2	pl.	*amalkaldik*	*waantamωk*
3	pl.	*amlakalditiš*	*waantamohettich*

		B.
2	sing.	okat
3	sing.	ŭnanĭsts-okas
1	pl. e.	nŏk-ok-ŭnanĭsts-okapinan
1	pl. i.	ŏk-ŭn-okauop
2	pl.	okak
3	pl.	ŭnanĭsts-okasau

The true imperative forms in the above tables, to a degree, exhibit a relationship with each other. In particular I point out the second person plural, which terminates in a gutteral in all dialects. The Ojibway forms with *ta-* and those of Cree with *kata-* belong rather to the future indicative. The third person forms of Micmac are forms of the conditional.

For examples of the transitive conjugation with an animate object, I choose O. *wābam* 'see him', C. *mowi* 'eat him', N. *wadchan* 'keep him' and B. *ŭkomĭmmĭs* 'love him'. For Micmac I have no suitable paradigms.

		O.	**C.**
2	sing.	wābam, wābamākan	mowi, mowim, mowākan
3	sing.	o-ga-wābamān	kata-mowew
1	pl. e.	wābamāda	mowātaw, mowākak, etc.
1	pl. i.		
2	pl.	wābamig	mowik, mowākek
3	pl.	o-ga-wābamāwan	kata-mowewok

[58]

	N.	**B.**
2 sing.	wadchan	ŭkomĭmmĭs
3 sing.	wadchanonch	ŭnanĭst-ŭkomĭmmŏsaie
1 pl. e.	} wadchanontah	ŭn-na-nŏk-ok-ŭn-ĭst-ŭkomĭmmŭnan
1 pl. i.		
2 pl.	wadchanók	ŭkomĭmmok
3 pl.	wadchanáhettich	ŭnanĭst-ŭkomĭmmŏsauaie

[J.S.: See footnote.⁶⁰]
Natick also has a form for the first person singular: *wadchanonti*. In these paradigms we also find the points of agreement that we notice in the intransitive conjugation. The Ojibway forms with *ga-* and the Cree forms with *kata-* are actually future indicatives.

In conclusion, I give further, examples of the transitive conjugation with an inanimate object: O. *wābandan* 'see it;, C. *sākita* 'love it', M. *šketen* 'obey it', N. *wadchanish* 'keep it', B. *ŭkometsit* 'love it'. I omit here the dual forms of Micmac.

	O.	**C.**
2 sing.	wābandan, wābandāmokan	sākita, sākitākan
3 sing.	o-ga-wābandān	kata-sākitaw

60.

		Micmac Imperitive from H&F 1990	**Endings from Dawe**
2	sing.	nmi (short i) 'see him, them'	-∅
3	sing.	nmiaj 'let him see him, them'	-ač (jussive)
1	pl. e.	nmianej 'let us see him, them'	not given
1	pl. i.	nmianej 'let us see him, them'	-aneč
2	pl.	nmikw '(you pl.) see him, them'	-kw
3	pl.	nmia'tij 'let them see him, them'	-a:tič (jussive)

		O.	**C.**
1	pl. e.	wābandānda	sākitātaw, sākitākak, etc.
1	pl. i.		
2	pl.	wābandamog	sākitāk, sākitākek
3	pl.	o-ga-wābandānawa	kata-sākitāwok

		M.	**N.**
2	sing.	šketen	wadchanish
3	sing.	šketš	wadchanitch
1	pl. e.	škedemutineš	wadchanumuttuh
1	pl. i.		
2	pl.	škedemutik	wadchanumωk
3	pl.	škedemutitiš	wadchanumahettich

		B.
2	sing.	ŭkometsit
3	sing.	ŭnanĭst-ŭkometsis
1	pl. e.	nŏk-ok-ŭnanĭst-ŭkometsipinan
1	pl. i.	ŏk-ŭnanĭst-ŭkometsip
2	pl.	ŭkometsĭk
3	pl.	ŭnanĭst-ŭkometsĭsau

After that which has been mentioned preceding the tables, these paradigms give no cause for special remarks.

[59]

Tenses

§ 46. Ojibway and Cree have the same tense system for which reason we shall discuss both of these dialects in relation with each other.

In Ojibway, one forms the **imperfect** from the present by the means of the suffix *-ban* (*-pan*), which we have already learned under the temporal inflexion of the noun. The personal terminations, which generally precede a preterite suffix, exhibit some peculiarities. We also find imperfect forms characterized by *-ban* (*-pan*) in Cree, but in most cases this dialect employs the equivalent suffix *-tai* (*-tā-*). Examples :

- O. *nind-ikkitonaban* 'I said': *nind-ikkit* 'I say'.
- O. *nin-wābamaban* 'I saw him': *nin-wābama* 'I see him'.
- O. *nin-wābandānaban* 'I saw it': *nin-wābandān* 'I see it'.
- O. *wābamagiban* 'if I had seen him': *wābamag* 'if I see him'.
- O. *wābandāmāmban* 'if I had seen it': *wābandāmān* 'if I see it'.
- C. *ni-nipānāpan, ni-nipātai* 'I slept': *ni-nipān* 'I sleep'.
- C. *ni-nipāt(ān)ān* 'we (excl.) slept': *ni-nipānān* 'we (excl.) sleep'.
- C. *sakihepan, o-sakihātai* 'he loved him': *sakihew* 'he loves him'.
- C. *nipāyāpan* 'if you (sing.) slept'. *nipāyan* 'if you sleep'.

It has to be remarked that the imperfect conjunctives of Ojibway have a pluperfect meaning.

The **perfect** is derived from the present by prefixing of O. *gī-* (mutated *gā-*) and C. *ki-*. Examples:

- O. *nin-gī-ikkit* 'I have said': *nind-ikkit* 'I say'.
- O. *nin-gī-wābama* 'I have seen him'.
- C. *ni-ki-nipan* 'I have slept': *ni-nipan* 'I sleep'.

The **pluperfect** is formed from the imperfect by adding the prefix just mentioned. Examples:

- O. *nin-gī-ikkitonaban* 'I had said': *nin-gī-ikkit* "I have said': *nind-ikkitonaban* 'I said'.
- C. *ni-ki-nipātai* 'I had slept': *ni-ki-nipān* 'I have slept': *ni-nipātai* 'I sleep'.

Apart from the third persons of the indicative, to which I shall soon return, the **future** is formed by the means of the prefix O. *ga-*, *gad-* (*gē-* and *gēd-* mutated), and C. *ka-* (*ke-* mutated). Examples:

- O. *nin-gad-ikkit* 'I shall say': *nind-ikkit* 'I say'.
- O. *nin-ga-wābama* 'I shall see him': *nin-wābama* "I see him'.
- C. *ni-ka-nipān* 'I shall sleep': *ni-nipān* 'I sleep'.

- C. *ni-ka-mowa* 'I shall eat him': *ni-mowaw* 'I eat him'.

The third person of the transitive indicative in Ojibway has the same prefix:

O. *o-ga-wābaman* 'he shall see him'

The third persons of the intransitive indicative in Ojibway have *ta-* as the prefix, which is *kata-* (*kita-*) in Cree for the intransitive and transitive indicative. Examples:

- O. *ta-ikkito* 'he shall say': *ikkito* ''he says'.
- C. *kata-nipaw* 'he shall sleep': *nipaw* 'he sleeps'.
- C. *kata-mowew* 'he shall eat him': *mowew* 'he eats him'.

In the future conjunctive of all persons we find O. *gē(d)-* and C. *ke-* the mutated form of O. *ga(d)-* and C. *ka-*:

- O. *gēd-ikkitoiān* 'that I shall say': *ikkitoiān* 'that I say'.
- O. *gēd-ikkitod* 'that he shall say': *ikkitod* 'that he says'.
- O. *gē-wābamag* 'that I shall see him': *wābamag* 'that I see him'.
- C. *ke-nipāyān* 'that I shall sleep': *nipāyān* 'that I sleep'.
- C. *ke-nipāt* 'that he shall sleep': *nipāt* 'that he sleeps'.

The **definite future** is acquired by providing the perfect with the future prefix. In the third persons of the indicative one uses O. *ta-* and C. *kata-* (*kita-*) where it is required. Examples:

- O. *nin-ga-gī-ikkit* 'I shall have said': *ni-gī-ikkit* 'I have said'.
- C. *ni-ka-ki-nipān* 'I shall have slept': *ni-ki-nipān* 'I have slept'.
- O. *ta-gī-ikkito* 'he shall have said': *gī-ikkito* 'he has said'.
- C. *kata-ki-nipaw* 'he shall have slept': *ki-nipaw* 'he has slept'.

In Cree one can also form the definite future from the pluperfect forms.

§ 47. Concerning the formation of the tenses in Micmac and Natick, they are not of the sort, that I could venture a systematic explanation. I must limit myself to stating some clearly recognizable facts.

Both languages have a preterite, which at least in Micmac can be labeled with the name of i m p e r f e c t, and which is marked by a *-p* suffix. Whether this suffix has something to do with the soon to be mentioned *-ben*(*-pen*) and the *-ban*(*-pan*) suffix of Ojibway and Cree spoken of in the previous paragraph, I dare not decide. Examples:

[61]
- M. *amalkayep* 'I danced': *amalkaye* 'I dance'.
- M. *amalkašep* 'you (sing.) danced': *amalkan* 'you (sing.) dance'.
- M. *šaktemep* 'I obeyed it': *šaktem* 'I obey it.
- M. *šaktemutiokšep* 'you (pl.) obeyed it': *šaktemutoik* 'you (pl.) obey it'.
- M. *delintutikušp* 'we (incl.) sang it': *delintutiku* 'we sing it'.
- N. *nωwaantamup* 'I was wise': *nωwaantam* 'I am wise'.
- N. *waantamup* 'he was wise': *waantamnoh* 'he is wise'.
- N. *nωwaantamumunnónup* 'we were wise': *nωwaantamumun* 'we are wise'.
- N. *nωwadchanóunonup* 'we kept him': *nωwadchanoun* 'we keep him'.
- N. *kωwadchanoup* 'you (pl.) kept him': *kωwadchanau* ;'you (pl.) keep him'.
- N. *ωwadchanumunap* 'he kept it': *ωwadchanumun* 'he keeps it'.
- N. *nωwadchanumumunnónup* 'we kept it'. *nωwadchanumumun* 'we keep it'.

In certain cases Micmac has a preterite formation with the suffix *-ek* that is also used in the temporal inflection of the noun. Examples: *amalkadek* 'when he danced': *amalkat* 'he dances', *amalkaldiokuek* 'when he danced': *amalkat* 'he dances', *amalkaldiokuek* 'when you (pl.) danced': *amalkaldiok* 'you (pl.) dance'.

The **perfect** in Micmac is formed from the imperfect by providing the prefix *kigi-* e.g., *kigi amalkayep* 'I have danced'. One acquires a **pluperfect** by further prefixing *kiš* to this *kigi*. It is not impossible that these prefixes are related to O. *gī-* and C. *ki*.

The **future** of Micmac has a *d* and moreover peculiar personal endings as characterizing elements.{k} Examples: *ideš* 'I shall be': *eim* 'I am', *amalkadeš* 'I shall dance': *amalkaye* 'I dance', *amalkadeks* 'you (sing.) shall dance': *amalkan* 'you (sing.) dance', *delintudeš* 'I shall sing it': *delintu* 'I sing it'. In contrast the future in Natick is formed by the means of a particle (*mos* and *pish*), which indicates the future.

The formation of the tenses for the conjunctive and the conditional in Micmac is not particularly clear. In certain preterite forms we find a *-ben(-pen)* element, which may be identical with O. C. *-ban(-pan)*. The combination *-še-ben* and the *-šen* that occurs beside it, also play a role in the temporal inflexion of the noun.

§ 48. Concerning Blackfoot, I only point out the formation of the tenses for the indicative. The temporal formations of the conjunctive etc. are completely variant and only the future of the potential is connected to that of the indicative.

The **present** indicative usually does not have anything other than the pronominal prefixes, but sometimes it is provided with an aspect-indicating prefix that is inserted between the pronominal elements and the verbal stem. The aspect-indicating prefixes are *ai-*, which has a momentary-durative and *au-*, which has an iterative-continuative meaning. These prefixes are not however exclusively bound to the present. For *ai-* it can be noticed that it is commonly infixed after the initial consonant or consonants of the verbal stem. For *ai-* as with *au-*, I only give a single example:

- *nit-ai-oka* 'I am sleeping at the moment'.
- *nit-au-auaiakiaki* 'I knock continually, I continue to knock':
- *nit-auaiakiaki* 'I knock'.

The present is also often used for past tense, but Blackfoot also has yet another **preterite** that is characterized by the prefix *sit(s-)*. Examples:

- *nit-sit-ŭkometŭkki* 'I loved'.
- *nit-sits-oka* 'I slept'.
- *nit-sit-ŭkometsip* 'I loved it'.

The inflection for the **perfect** is *kåk* or *kai*, of which the later is reminiscent of the previously mentioned forms O. *gī-* and C. *ki*. Perhaps there is a true etymological connection. Examples:

- *ni-kåk-ŭkometŭkki* 'I have loved'.
- *ni-kai-oka* 'I have slept'.
- *ni-kåk-ŭkomĭmmau* 'I have loved him'.

The **future** is characterized by *ak(s)-*, which does not seem to be connected with the prefixes of the other languages. Examples:

- *nit-ak-ŭkometŭkki* 'I shall love'.
- *nit-aks-oka* 'I shall sleep'.
- *ak-ŭkometsĭmaie* 'he shall love it'.[61]

---

61. The conjunctive, which is characterized by a suffix *-s(i)* or *-χs(i)* and personal endings, forms a special final conjunctive from the simple conjunct by means of the prefix *aχk(s)-* or *aχkit(s)-*. These prefixes may also be attached to the indicative to

Incorporation

§ 49. To a great extent, the pronouns with subject and object meanings are either actually incorporated or thought of as virtually present in the verb of the Algonquian languages. Incorporation of other case functions with the pronoun is also not foreign to this language family. The prefixes are identical or closely related to the separate personal pronouns (see § 24), in contrast, the suffixes exhibit a great diversity and are not at all connected to the inseparable personal pronouns. Pluralization of incorporated elements - even when these are prefixed - are never made known except in the verbal ending. Dualization is only present in Micmac. Concerning the third person, it is to be noticed that there is also an indefinite third-person-subject in use in Algonquian, but I have not taken these up in my paradigms. Yet I am reminded of the previously mentioned reflexivity of the subordinated third persons, but in the verbal form. To give an idea of the Algonquian incorporation system, I shall cite some examples from the several languages. Perhaps it shall later become possible to reconstruct the incorporation of Proto-Algonquian by a full comparison of all forms in a range of dialects and then to analyze the reconstructed forms, up to a certain point, in their components.

Ojibway.

- *nind-inendam* 'I think', *nind-inendamin* 'we[62] think'.
- *kid-ikkit* 'you (sing.) say', *kid-ikkitom* 'you (pl.) say'.
- *dagwišin* 'he arrives', *dagwišinog* 'they arrive'.
- *dagwišinim* 'one arrives'.
- *nin-wābama* 'I see him', *nin-wābamānan* 'we[63] see him'. *nin-wābamag* 'I see them', *nin-wābamānanig* 'we[64] see them'.

---

create a semantic final. They can also prefix to verbal nouns in *-ani* transforming them into a third specially characterized final conjunct.

The subjunctive is completely suppositional and does not have the type of past tense given above for the conjunctive although both the conjunctive and subjunctive have an indefinite passive, which must be omitted here for the sake of brevity.

As above, the conjunctive and subjunctive form the future by means of ak(s). For the conjunctive the forms are in n-ak-, k-ak-, and m-ak-. For the subjunctive, forms are in m-ak- for all persons (see Uhlenbeck's BG 1938).

62. (excl.)
63. (excl.)
64. (excl.)

- *o-wābamān* 'he sees him', *o-wābamāwan* 'they see him', *o-wābamān* 'he sees them', *o-wābamāwan* 'they see them'.
- *nin-wābamimān ōsan* 'I see his father', *nin-wābamimānan ōsan* 'we[65] see his father'.
- *ki-wābamin* 'I see you (sing.)', *ki-wābamininim* 'I see you (pl.)'.
- *ki-wābamigo* 'you (sing.) are seen', *ki-wābamigomin* 'you (pl.) are seen'.
- *ki-wābam* 'you (sing.) see me', *ki-wābamim* 'you (pl.) see me'.
- *ki-wābamimin* 'you (sing.) see us', 'you (pl.) see us'.
- *nin-wābamigo* 'I am seen', *nin-wābamigomin* 'we[66] are seen'.
- *nin-wābandān* 'I see it', *nin-wābandāmin* 'we[67] see it', *nin-wābandānan* 'I see them (i.)', *nin-wābandāmin* 'we[68] see them (i.)'.
- *o-wābandān* 'he sees it', *o-wābandānawa* 'they see it', *o-wābandānan* 'he sees them (i.)', *o-wābandānawan* 'they see them (i.)', *wābandām* 'one sees it'.

Cree.

- *ni-nipān* 'I sleep', *ni-nipānan* 'we[69] sleep'.
- *nipaw* 'he sleeps', *nipawok* 'they sleep'.
- *nipāliwa, nipāyiwa* 'his (e.g., father) sleeps', 'his (e.g., parents) sleep'.
- *nipāmākan* 'it sleeps', *nipāmākanwa* 'they (i.) sleep'. [64]
- *nipāmākaniliw* 'his (e.g., body) sleeps', *nipāmākaniliwa, nipāmākaniyiwa* 'his (e.g., eyes) sleep'.
- *nipāniwiw, nipāniwan* 'one sleeps'.
- *ki-mowaw* 'you (sing.) eat him', *ki-mowāwaw* 'you (plur.) eat him'.
- *ki-mowāwok* 'you (sing.) eat them', *ki-mowāwāwok* 'you (plur.) eat them'.
- *ni-sākihimawa* 'I love his (e.g., daughter)'.
- *ki-mowik* 'he eats you (sing.)', *ki-mowikwok* 'they eat you (sing.)'.
- *ki-mowikowaw* 'he eats you (pl.)', *ki-mowikowāwok* 'they eat you (pl.)'.
- *ki-mowitin* 'I eat you (sing.)', *ki-mowitinān* 'we[70] eat you (sing.)'.
- *ki-mowin* ' you (sing.) eat me', *ki-mowinān* 'you (sing.) eat us'.

---
65. (excl.)
66. (excl.)
67. (excl.)
68. (excl.)
69. (excl.)
70. (excl.)

- *kit-ošitowin* 'you (sing.) make him for me'.
- *kit-ošitwātin* 'I make him for you (sing.)'.
- *ni-wāpaten* 'I see it', *ni-wāpatenān* 'we[71] see it'.
- Micmac.
- *eim* 'I am', *eimek* 'we (excl.) are', *eimuku* 'we (incl.) are'.
- *ygan* 'you (sing.) push', *ygayok* 'you (pl.) push'.
- *amalkat* 'he dances', *amalkagik* 'they both dance', *amalkaldigik* 'they dance'.
- *šaktem* 'I obey it', *šaktemek* 'we both (excl.) obey it', *šaktemuku* 'we both (incl.) obey it', *šaktemutiek* 'we (excl.) obey it', *šaktemutiku* 'we (incl.) obey it'.
- *delintok* 'he sings it', *delintutiš* 'they both sing it', *delintutigik* 'they sing it'.
- *euikemuin* 'you (sing.) write me abot it', *euikemuinel* 'you (sing.) write me about them (i.)'.
- *euikemul* 'I write you (sing.) about it', *euikemulanel* 'I write you (sing.) about them (i.)'.
- *euikemuagel* 'he writes him (them (a.)) about it (them (i.))'.
- *menatul* 'I take it off of you (sing.)', *menatulanel* 'I take them (i.) off of you (sing.)'.

Natick.

- *nωwaantam* 'I am wise', *nωwaantamumun* 'we[72] are wise'.
- *nωwadchan* 'I keep him', *nωwadchanoun* 'we[73] keep him', *nωwadchanóog* 'I keep them', *nωwadchanóunonog* 'we[74] keep them'.
- *kωwadchansh* 'I keep you (sing.)', *kωwadchanunumun* 'we[75] keep you (sing.)', *kωwadchanunumwω* 'I keep you (pl.)', *kωwadchanunumun* 'we[76] keep you (plur.)'.
- *kωwadchaneh* 'you (sing.) keep me', *kωwadchanimwω* 'you (plur.) keep me', *kωwadchanimun* 'you (sing.) keep us'[77], 'you (pl.) keep us[78]'.

---

71. (excl.)
72. (excl.)
73. (excl.)
74. (excl.)
75. (excl.)
76. (excl.)
77. (excl.)
78. (excl.)

- *nωwadchanumun* 'I keep it', *nωwadchanumumun* 'we[79] keep it'. [65]

Blackfoot.

- *nit-ai-oka* 'I sleep', *nit-ai-okapinan* 'we[80] sleep'.
- *kit-ŭkomĭmmau* 'you (sing.) love him', *kit-ŭkomĭmmauau* 'you (pl.) love him', *kit-ŭkomĭmmaiau* 'you (sing.) love them', *kit-ŭkomĭmmauaksau* 'you (pl.) love them'.
- *nit-ŭkomĭmmok* 'he loves me', *nit-ŭkomĭmmaukiau* 'they love me'.
- *kit-ŭkomĭmmo* 'I love you (sing.)', *kit-ŭkomĭmmopauu* 'I love you (pl.)'.
- *nit-ŭkometsip* 'I love it', *nit-ŭkometsipan* 'we[81] love it'.
- *ŭkometsĭmaie* 'he loves it', *ŭkometsĭmiau* 'they love it'.
- *ŭkometsĭminaai* 'he loves it of him'.

The **incorporation of the nouns**, which phenomenon I can only illustrate by examples from Ojibway and Cree, is not as broad as the incorporation of the pronouns in the verbal form:

- O. *nandomikwe*, C. *nandawamiskwew* 'he hunts beavers': O. *amīk*, C. *amisk* 'beaver': O. *o-nandonēwān*, C. *nandonawew* 'he seeks him'.
- O. *pāginindži* 'he has a swollen hand': *onindž* 'his hand': *pāgiši* (a.), *pāgišin* (i.) is swollen'.

In the treatment of mood representation and of the tenses, we have seen that the verb of the Algonquian languages has all sorts of affixes, which are bound to the verb stem in a more or less inseparable manner. It has however not yet been discussed that these languages also possess many other prefixes, which modify the meaning of the verb. A portion of these prefixes is reminiscent of our **pre-verbs.** In a more comprehensive work on the Algonquian languages one paragraph should be dedicated to the pre-verbs, but in this provisional sketch I deem it is sufficient to bring attention to their presence.

---

79. (excl.)
80. (excl.)
81. (excl.)

Secondary verbs

§ 50. In closing, some words on the several sorts of secondary verbs in Ojibway. In the remaining languages one also finds similarly derived verbs, but I shall only systematically treat those of Ojibway, since I do not have complete data for any other language at my service. Finally, however, I will draw a bit nearer to Cree, to show how close the relationship between both languages is with regard to the formation of derived verbs.

The **reflexives** and **reciprocols** have already been treated in § 35. At this time the following categories remain yet to be mentioned:

- **Accomodatives**, e.g., *nind-ožitamawa* 'I make it for him', *od-ožitamawān* 'he makes it for him': *nind-ožiton* 'I make it', *od-ožiton* 'he makes it'; *o-nibōtāwan* 'he dies for him': *nibō* 'he dies'. The actual object of these verbs is the person whom one does some thing for.
- **Causatives**, e.g., *nin-wābandaa* 'I make him see it': *nin-wābandān* 'I see it'; *nin-widigea* 'I make him marry': *nin-widige* 'I am married'.
- **Frequentatives**, e.g., *nin-papakitēwa* 'I strike him repeatedly',: *nin-pakitēwa* 'I strike him'; *nin-tatāngiškawa* 'I kick him repeatedly': *nin-tāngiškawa* 'I kick him'. These verbs frequently have mutated reduplicated vowel, e.g., *nin-gāgigit* ' I speak long and much': *nin-gigit* 'I speak'; *nin-pāpindige* 'I come in often': *nin-pindige* 'I come in'; *nin-nānibaw* 'I stand here and there': *nin-nibaw* 'I stand'. The original meaning of these verbs is distributive, from which fundamental idea the notions of frequentative and intensive have developed.
- **Excessives**, e.g., *nin-nibāšk* 'I sleep too much', *nibāški* 'he sleeps too much': *nin-nibā* 'I sleep', *nibā* 'he sleeps'; *nin-minikwēšk* 'I drink too much', *minikwēški* 'he drinks too much': *nin-minikwē* 'I drink', *minikwē* 'he drinks'.
- **Commiseratives**, *nin-bakadēš* 'I, poor wretch, am hungry', *bakadēši* 'he is hungry, the poor wretch': *nin-bakadē* 'I am hungry', *bakadē* 'he is hungry'; *nind-ākosiš* 'I, the wretch, am sick', *ākosiši* 'he is sick, the wretch': *nind-ākos* 'I am sick', *ākosi* 'he is sick'.
- **Simulatives**, e.g., *nin-nibākās* ' I pretend to sleep', *nibākāso* 'he pretends to sleep': *nin-nibōkās* 'I feign dying': *nin-nib* 'I die', *nibō* 'he dies'.
- I include here some denominative categories:

- **Essives**, e.g., *nind-ininiw* 'I am a man', *ininiwi* 'he is a man': *inini* 'man'; *nin-wābiganiw* 'I am clay', *wābiganiwi* 'he is clay': *wābigan* 'clay'; *bāpiwiniwan* 'he is laughing': *bāpiwin* 'laughter; laughing'.
- **Abundative**, e.g., *anisinābeka* 'there are many Indians': *anisinābe* 'Indian'; *nibika* 'there is much water'.
- **Possessives**, e.g., *nind-otšimān* 'I have a canoe', *otšimāni* 'he has a canoe': *tšimān* 'canoe'; *nind-omitig* 'I have a tree', *omitigo* 'he has a tree': *mitig* 'tree'. [67]
- **Productives** e.g., *nin-mikanāke* 'I make a road': *mikana* 'road'; *nind-iškotēke* 'I make fire': *iškotē* 'fire'.

Variations of the above mentioned formations can also be pointed out in Cree. Accomodatives are, for example *nit-ošitamāwaw* 'I make it for him' (=O. *nind-ožitamawa*), *ni-nipustamāwaw* 'I die for him' (cf. O. *ni-nibōtawa*). Cree also has causatives, e.g., *ni-wāpatehaw* 'I make it so that he sees it' (cf. O. *nin-wābandaa*). Just as in Ojibway, there are duplicated verbs with intensive meaning in Cree and also the simulatives in *-kās(o)* are a common feature of both languages. Examples of essives are *nāpewiw* 'he is a man', *iskwewiw* 'she is a woman' and the exclusive inanimate essive suffix *-iwan* is also present here. Abundatives in Cree have the ending *-skaw*, e.g., *nipiskaw* 'there is much water' (=O. *nibika*). The possessives and the productives of Ojibway also correspond to the formation of the verbs in Cree in a related manner. Still another interesting category of the secondary verbs is that of the diminutives, out of which, as we have seen under § 37 the negative conjugation of Ojibway has developed.

Appendix

... on secondary verbs [J.S.]

The secondary verbs make up a portion of what is sometimes referred to as secondary derivation. Secondary derivation also includes features such as diminutives, pejoratives §18 and the formation of verbal abstracts §19, but these have already been treated.

In Micmac "a number of verbs are formed from nouns by the addition of -*i* or -*mi*, the first ending replacing our verb 'be' and the second our verb 'have', when joined to nouns, pronouns or adjectives, which are all conjugated like *teluisi*." (see H&F 1990) Verbs can also be formed from the verbal abstract forms treated under §19 by again adding -*i*, -*in*, -*it*" (first, second and third persons respectively) ": -*ik* in the third person inanimate signifies: there are some; there are none: *wisqîsuti, wisqîsutik*, 'there is illness'; *mu wisqîsutinukw, wisqîsuaqninukw*, 'there is none'." H&F 1990.

Natick Examples:

- Accomadatives: |-nuhsh| "makes TA stems from AI stems and extended TI themes, denoting action done on behalf of the object" Examples: *kishkoohoowannishonnat* 'to pay for him', *wuttatepantamonishshuh* 'he cares for (it) for them'
- Causatives: |-h| makes TA stems and |-ht| makes TI2 stems "from AI stems and extended TI themes" Examples: *nuttohquenitteham* 'I joined them in marriage', *wannehtouwahhinnummuk* 'if you (sg.) are made to lose it' from *noowanehtauunan* 'we (excl.) lose it', *kωwadchanumwahunan* 'I cause thee to keep him'.
- Essives: |-i-| and |-uwi-| form AI and II verbs of being. "|-i-| is used after noun stems ending in a |w| preceded by a vowel, and |-uwi-| after stems of other shapes. AI verbs from stems in vowel + |w|: *ahtoskauow* 'he is a chief man'," *manidtωω* 'he is God', *sontimmoω* 'he is chief'. "II from stem in |y|: *ayeahkeyeuuk* 'as long as the earth exists'.
- Possesssives: prefix |wu-| and suffix |-i-| forms AI verbs of possession that take a secondary object. "The prefix |wu-| is treated like the third-person prefix, inserting |t| before the initial vowel of an independent noun; dependant nouns beginning with |ē| have the prefix in the form |uw-| and those beginning with |ω| prefix |wut-|. The stems of verbs of possession that begin with |u-| (the regular treatment of |wu-| before certain

consonants) are treated as though they began with underlying |wu-| and hence take pronominal prefixes with contraction to |ω| and have |wá-| with initial change. Examples: *ootooshinneah* 'he has him as his father' from *noosh* 'my father', *omittumwis[sis]sinnapoh* 'he had her as his wife' from *ummittummmussissoh* 'his wife', "*othiheun* 'he owns it; it belongs to him' lit. 'he has it as his property' from *wutihe* 'his property', *wa-Mannittoomitcheg* '(those) who have (him as) God' (the hyphen is only to preserve the customary capitalization) from *ummannittωmoh* 'his God'.
- Productives: |-uht^{e}á-| forms AI verbs of making and so forth. Example: *waque ahtukanehteapah* 'as far as she formerly made the field' from *ohteuk* 'field' (stem |aht^{e}uhkôni-|) (Natick material is drawn or reproduced from G&B 1988) .

Blackfoot Examples:
- Accomadatives: In Blackfoot most accomodatives are formed by means of the suffix -*mo* or -*to-mo*- e.g: *nitáikakomoau* 'I chop for him/her' from *nitáikakiaki* 'I chop',
- *nitástamoau* 'I hammer in for him/her' from *nitástaki* 'I hammer in', *nitáuatomoau* 'I eat for him/her' from *nitáuyi* 'I eat', *nitáisikstomoau* 'I bite for him/her' from *nitáisikstaki* 'I bite'. Ther are irregularly formed accomodatives as well: *nitáinoχtoau* 'I boil for him/her' from *nitáinixt* 'I boil', *nitáixketoau* 'I cook for him/her' from *nitáixket* 'I cook', *nitáisαpiau* 'I look for him/her' from *nitáisαpi* 'I look', *nitáuyiau* 'I cook for him/her' from *nitáuyosi* 'I cook'.
- Causatives-Permissives: Causatives-Permissives are formed from intransitive stems by means of the suffix -*ats*-, they then take the transitive animate endings e.g.: *kitsíkstakiatso* 'I make you bite (I let you bite)', *nitsíkstakiatsau* 'I make him/her bite (I allow him/her to bite').
- Causatives Proper: The Causatives proper is characterized by the suffix -(*i*)*pi*- e.g.:
  - *ki aitotsípiuaei* 'and then he brought him/her there',
  - *nisótαmitotsìpiòko* 'then I was brought there' (both from *oto*- 'to come to, to go to').
- Frequentatives-Exessives: The only Frequentatives given in Uhlenbeck's Blackfoot Grammar are used in an unfavorable sense and might be considered Exessives. The suffix is -(*e*)*pitsi*: *epúyepitsiu* 'talks away, has the bad habit of talking too much' from *áipuyiu* 'talks', *asáiniepitsiu* 'cries always, has the annoying habit of crying' from *áuasainiu* 'cries (weeps)',

áitskàpitsiu 'is always fighting, has the bad habit of fighting' from *áiskau* 'fights'.
- Transformative: The Transfomative is characterized by the suffix *-àsi-*, e.g., *matápiuàsiu* 'turns into a person' (*matápi* 'person'), *akéuàsiu* 'turns into a woman' (*àké* 'woman'), *mistsísàsiu* 'turns into a tree (turns into wood)' (*mistsís* 'tree, log, stick, piece of wood').
- Possessives: "The possessive verbs are ordinarily derived, not immediately from the noun-stem, but from the possessive noun-form of the third person, and designate, with intransitive endings, that one possesses the person or thing expressed by the noun, or, with transitive endings, that one has somebody or thing in the function of that person or thing. In certain cases, principally or exclusively in the third person (and fourth person based thereon) the *o-* of the possessive noun-form is substituted by *i-* (*e-*), but after a prefix we find, even in such cases, the *o* restored. Where the possessive noun-form of the third person has *u-* instead of *o-*, the substitution of the possessive prefix by *i-* (*e-*) never occurs." Uhlenbeck's BG from 1938 pp 146 e.g., *nítoχkoyi* 'I have a son', *oχkóyiu* 'he has a son', *nitáuχkoyimau* 'I have him as a son (for a son)', *áuχkoyimiu* 'he has him as a son (for a son)': *oχkói* 'his son. *nitúnni* 'I have a father', *únniu* 'he has a father', *nitúnnimau, nitáunimau* 'I have him as a father (for father)', *áunimiu* 'he has him as a father (for father)': *únni* 'his father'. *nitoksístsi* 'I have a mother', *iksístsiu* (*-oksístsiu*) 'he has a mother': *oksístsi* 'his mother'. There are however different types of possessive verbs, e.g., *otoχkáuotànis* 'because he has got a shield', *nimátopìmixp* 'I had no rope' (cf. *áuotàni* 'shield and *apïs* 'rope' *nitópim* 'my rope').
- Productives: Productives are characterized by the suffix *-ka-* e.g., *nitáitsikixk* 'I make moccasins', *áitsikixkau* 'he makes moccasins': *matsikín, atsikín* 'moccasin', *áietaχkau* 'he makes a saddle':*eétan* (*iítan*) 'saddle'), *áinamaχkau* 'he makes a gun': *námau* 'gun', *áukspikainàmaχkau* 'he makes a (sticky) bow': *akspíkainàma* '(sticky) bow'.

Material drawn from Uhlenbeck 1938.

End notes

... on the translation [J.S.]

a I have chosen to systematically represent the Dutch word "Waarderingsklassen" (literally, "classes of appreciation or worth") as "gender" to reflect the successful contemporary employment of this term on a rather large scale. The words that I have consistently translated as "animate" and "inanimate" are actually "bezield" and "onbezield" roughly "besouled" and "unbesouled" in English.

b I have chosen to employ "obviative" and "subobviative" based on contemporary usage however 'subordinated' and 'double subordinated' are more literal translations of the Dutch words. It should be noted that a rather large array of terms are and have been employed to represent this grammatical feature, of which 'proximate person' and 'fourth person' should be mentioned.

c In Baraga's dictionary he glosses this as 'one who prays as a Christian' I am not certain of the word's traditional (pre-Christian) use or meaning.

d Uhlenbeck was quite accomplished in the field of Indo-European linguistics (See Eggermont-Molenaar and Van Berkel Montana (2005: 9) and Genee and Hinrichs 2008/2009). He could not have been completely ignorant that similar anomalies existed in those languages as well, for example in the Germanic languages the words for 'sun' and 'night' are historically feminine while the words for 'moon' and 'day' are historically masculine. Furthermore 'street', which is almost unquestionably inanimate or neuter, has synonyms in masculine and feminine genders (masculine *der Weg*, feminine die Strasse, die Gasse and die Bahn).

e Baraga's dictionary glosses O. *nika* as 'a kind of wild goose'.

f This short paragraph is tricky and appears in the original French/Dutch as follows:

- *mokueš Inuinu* 'point d'homme' bij *Inu* 'mensch'.
- *mu šabuguaninu* 'point d'eau'; *mu šabuguaninugul* 'point d'eaux' bij *šabiguan* 'water'.

Thanks to Joe Wilmot we have two comparable forms from Listuguj dialect:

- *mokueš Inuinu* corresponds to Listuguj *moqwa' 'Nnuinu* 'not one of us' and *mu šabuguaninugul* corresponds to *mu samqwaninugul* 'they

contain no water' or 'they are not wet'; more like 'they have no water on them`(i).
g G&B 1988 has the following to say about TA themes. "The transitive animate uses four theme signs to make the four TA themes, each of which specifies particular combinations of persons as the subject and object:
  - Theme 1 (direct theme) |-ô|, higher status acting on animate lower status;
  - Theme 2 (inverse theme) |-ukw|, lower status acting on higher status;
  - Theme 2a (passive theme) |-it\u1d49á|, indefinite acting on first or second person;
  - Theme 3 |-i|, second person on first;
  - Theme 4 |-un|, first person on second."
  For more on the theme signs see G&B 1988 for Massachusett and Valentine 2001 for Ojibway.
h The following sentence is taken from G&B 1988 under TI "Each of the four TI stem classes has a different theme sign: TI-1a |-am|; TI-1b |-um|; TI-2 |-aw|; TI-3 |-∅|.
i I have translated the Dutch word "vormleer" as grammar both here and in the title, but it could also be translated as morphology.
j In Listuguj (Restigouche) dialect this *i* is a u as in *nemu'gw* 'If we see him/her' and 'you (pl.) see him/them'. In Listuguj dialect *mu nemi'gw* is 'if s/he does not see me' (emendation from Joe Wilmot).
k The paradigms given here, which provide the rest of the personal endings, are reproduced from "The Mi'kmaq Future: An Analysis by Stephanie Inglis and Eleanor Johnson. It can be seen below that this material uses an unvoiced *t* where Uhlenbeck's sources apparently used a voiced *d*.

   AI future Endings and AI Future of verb stem -*np*- 'to sleep'
   Endings Stem + Endings
   -*tes npates* 'I will sleep'
   -*tesk/-teks npateks* 'You (sg.) will sleep'
   -*tew npatew* 'S/he will sleep'
   -*tesnu/-teksnu npate(k)snu* 'We incl. will sleep'
   -*tesnen/-teksnen npate(k)snen* 'We excl. will sleep'
   -*toqsîp npatoqsîp* 'You (pl.) will sleep'
   -*taq npataq* 'They will sleep'

   For an historical perspective and the Etymology of these morphemes, the original article from which these tables were drawn should be consulted.

www.ingramcontent.com/pod-product-compliance
Lightning Source LLC
Chambersburg PA
CBHW051405290426
44108CB00015B/2159